From the Blitz to Beeching

Memories of a Wiltshire Railway Signalman

The author in Chippenhan East signal box

From the Blitz to Beeching

Memories of a Wiltshire Railway Signalman

By Bob Jones

ELSP

Published in 2022 by Rachel Gough

Origination by Ex Libris Press
www.ex-librisbooks.co.uk

Printed by TPM Ltd.
Farrington Gurney
Somerset

ISBN 978-1-912020-18-8

With thanks to my wife, daughter and friend Derek without whose
help this book would not have been written. Also thanks to the
late Michael B. Sadler who provided many of the photographs.
Thanks also to Craig Ryan for the book's title and Roger Jones
of Ex Libris Press for his invaluable help.

Dedication
To all the men and women past, present and future
who keep the trains running through Wiltshire.

Cover: Chippenham East signal box – my favourite signal box

CONTENTS

My Early Life

I was born in Ivy Cottage now number 98 Studley Corner on the 16 February 1926 at 3.15 p.m. my twin sister Rosemary was not born until the next day between midnight and 1 p.m. so we have different birthdays. When I was very young we moved to Derry Hill, however many years later my father's sister my Auntie Ada and her husband Uncle Bill lived in Ivy Cottage so I became familiar with the cottage and it was good to walk round and think to myself 'I was born here'.

Long before I was born my father David Robert Jones, also known as Bob had started working for the Great Western Railway. This was around 1913 and he was initially employed as a rail packer.

During the World War 1 he attested for military service on 1 December 1915 (4 days after getting married), initially he was a reservist and was eventually mobilised on 6 May 1916 and was posted to the 8th Battalion The Worcester Regiment. After training through the summer he departed from Southampton arriving at Rouen on 16 September 1916 and was involved in the Battle of the Somme from 26 September 1916. In March 1917 he was transferred to the 113th Railway Company, Royal Engineers, presumably because of his peace time occupation with the Great Western Railway. On 16 September 1917 he was certified as a skilled platelayer and in May 1919 he was classed as superior and over time his rank originally that of Sapper became Lance Corporal and Corporal. (Sources: British Army World War 1 Service Records WRO 363; War Diary April 1915 to October 1917 1/8 Battalion Worcestershire Regiment WO-95-2759-2 held at The National Archives, Kew)

On returning to England in September 1919 he worked as a lengthman in the gang working on the Calne Branch of the Great Western Railway through the 1920s. One very wet weekend in March 1930 he was taking part in the relaying of track at Melksham Station with other gangs. His clothing not like today's issue was soon completely saturated through. He became poorly and developed pneumonia and unfortunately died, he was aged 37. It was suspected that weekend had a part to play in his demise. As he died when I was only aged 4, I did not have the opportunity to discuss work with him; however I became interested in the railway system.

Calne branch permanent way gang, 1920s, probably near Black Dog siding. They are left to right: T Baker, R Jefferies, J Brittain, B Brittain, David Robert (Bob) Jones my father, C Dobson, G Robbins

Shortly after my father died we moved to 8 Old Derry Hill, a semi-detached cottage. It had one bedroom, a landing, living room, kitchen, and a lean to at the back of the house. The water-toilet was outside attached to the house, as there was no water laid on; all our waste water went down the toilet along with seven other houses. We had to fetch our drinking water from a tap across the road which was very slow running, as it came from a spring up in the woods about half mile away. We called it the fountain, there was a large round bowl about 3ft high and 3ft 6ins in dimension and over the top it was covered by a stone tile roof supported by a number of wooden posts and there was a painted inscription all round the inside:

'Here quench your thirst and make in me
An emblem of true charity,
Who why my Bounty bestow,
Am neither heard nor seen to flow.
Repaid by fresh supplies from Heaven,
For every cup of water given.'

My mother bought two small buckets for me and I had the job of carrying the water, it was said two buckets gives a better balance, it was a long way to carry the water 150 yards or so to the opposite side of the road. The neighbours seem to meet up there and lots of chattering went on while waiting for our buckets to fill.

A ditch ran down the back of the garden into a drain, which we had to keep clean, as it was liable to overflow. If it got blocked the water would run down the garden to our front door, which being lower at that point would let the water come into the house.

On the other side of the hedge running alongside the house was a drive to a field, which was also a right of way, so I also had to keep this clear.

I remember the steam wagons called Sentinels operated by Wootten Brothers. They used to stop outside to get up steam to power them up the Old Derry Hill. The drivers would talk to me so I would always go out to them. They used to call me 'artful'.

Mother, my twin sister Rosie, my older sister Ivy and I would go up to Gran and Grandfather's at number 40 Derry Hill, I remember I used to get tired by about 7 o'clock, so would take myself home and put myself to bed. On other occasions we all went home together, halfway down Old Derry Hill on the right above the wall was Cuckoo House which is no longer there. At that time it was lived in by Mr and Mrs Haddrell we always called out 'goodnight' winter or summer. On dry evenings in summer we would have a chat with them.

I spent many hours at the Automobile Association telephone box, which was situated at the bottom of Old Derry Hill on the junction with the A4. The AA man would be there quite often coming on his motorbike and sidecar. I was pleased to find that the Derry Hill AA telephone box no. 45 has been preserved and is currently in The National Telephone Kiosk Collection at Avoncroft Museum, Stoke Heath, Bromsgrove, Worcestershire.

Coming home from School, I would make my way to where I knew Granddad (William Cleverly) would be working in the woods, having asked previously where I could find him. The first thing I did was look in his frail, strawbay or nosebag for titbits of food and coffee, I knew my way all over the Bowood estate.

Sometimes I would walk with Granddad when he had to deliver rent notices to farmers in Hazeland and Bremhill for the Bowood Estate. He knew his way around everywhere. Collections for the rent were made on certain days at the Lansdowne Inn, Derry Hill, Dumbpost Inn in Bremhill, and The George Inn in Sandy Lane. He was doorman on these occasions. Rents were traditionally due on Lady Day - 25 March, Midsummer - Day 24 June, Michaelmas - 29 September, Christmas Day - 25 December, so I expect the collections dates were close to these dates. Another of his jobs was to collect money owing for the sale of wood.

There was no electricity or gas, oil lamps and candles were the only lighting we had. A Valor oil stove, which was a twin burner, was used for cooking. We had a small oven to put on the top to cook cakes, there was also a range in the kitchen.

My sister Rosie and I were always together; we spent lots of time with Auntie Ada and Uncle Bill who at that time lived at No. 13 Old Derry Hill. Auntie Ada made a good deal of fuss over us as they had no children of their own, later they moved to our old home at Studley.

The night watchman Mr Carpenter who worked for Wiltshire County Council had a little hut with a brazier to keep him warm during the night, this happened when there were road works on the hill. I used to spend time with him until my mother and sisters returned home. Some of the attraction was to have some of his bread pudding, which I can taste now.

Once a year in summer time we were invited to Bowood House for a party arranged by the Marquis of Lansdowne. We were picked up from school in the estate lorry by Mr Jim Stewart and taken to the house where the party was held in the Orangery. Lady Lansdowne welcomed us and a good tea was served. We were each given a gift to bring home; I remember one of my gifts was a torch. Later we were allowed outside to play in the gardens. My cousin David on one occasion fell into the lily pond; he was duly dried out and dressed in Lady Elizabeth's clothes to go home.

Christmas was spent at the cottage at Home Farm where my mother's brother Tom lived. There was limited space so we slept on the floor in the loft. It was great spending Christmas with Auntie Florrie and Uncle Tom and my three cousins Peter, Ken and David.

When I was quite young my sisters, mum and I developed scarlet fever, and we were taken to the fever hospital in Calne (where St Mary's Girls School, a private school is now) in a horse drawn fever wagon. All I can remember of all this was hearing the clip clop of the horse's hoofs, no siren in those days. This wagon eventually was used as a shepherd's hut on Blackland Downs.

I attended the village school in Derry Hill. From school we took nature walks around Bowood estate, and Miss Binns our teacher set us the task of finding as many different wild flowers as we could. The person who had the most was rewarded with some chocolate

We had a pet jackdaw which was taken from the nest, I made a box for him in a bush by the house door and he would follow us from tree to tree down to school. On Sunday he would come with us to Sunday school at Studley at the Methodist Chapel. Small objects, which he took a fancy to, would be taken into his box. Once I found my identity card tucked in the box, thankfully that was recovered. Soldiers came and setup camp in the park at the back of us, (we had then moved to 40 Derry Hill living with my grandparents William and Sarah Cleverly) and they were very interested in the jackdaw; after they had up sticks, we never saw the bird again, it was a very sad day indeed.

Just before the World War 2 there was lots of troop movement from Salisbury Plain most of the soldiers had walked all the way, although there were horses and mules pulling the guns and cooking wagons. We could smell the cooking as they were on the move. We picked some apples to give to the soldiers as they went by, they were so pleased.

One year there was a glut of chestnuts on the Bowood estate, the cattle were eating so many it was making them ill. The school was asked if some of the children would pick up as many as possible. We went into the park to the area called the Clumps near one of the entrances to the house. In the Clumps were a number of chestnut trees, which were causing the problem with the cattle. We children had great fun picking and filling up our bags. A lot of these trees were blown down in a gale that we had a few years ago, along with many more trees on the estate. That particular gale left some very sad sights in the woodland area.

We enjoyed Sunday School Anniversary. My Aunt Ada always polished our pennies with Brasso metal polish until they shone beautifully. It was a very special day. We looked forward to the Sunday School New Year Party in the schoolroom at Studley Methodist Chapel. When we came in the smell of the jellies and other foods was overwhelming. The Christmas tree decorations where still up and looked lovely especially when the electricity arrived and we could have fairy lights.

Before the electricity came it was oil lamps, therefore it was not so bright and cheerful. We played games having always to be careful of the Tortoise stove in the middle of the room. We all received an orange and a present off the tree.

Although we moved to Derry Hill when I was 4 we still continued to go to Studley Methodist Chapel. If it poured with rain on a Sunday morning we would go to Derry Hill Methodist Church Sunday School which was nearby instead. At Studley Chapel I remember Mr Fortune the Sunday School Superintendent at prayer time; he would take his handkerchief spread it on the floor and kneel down on one knee. The Congregation at Church could pay a rent for their place I think it was 1s.6d (7½p) a year or maybe quarterly. During the war the evening service was held in the Schoolroom, as the windows were easier to blackout.

When I left school at the age of 14 in 1940 I went to work at Home Farm at Bowood, I had considered applying for a car mechanic apprenticeship at a local garage like my cousin Peter, but apprenticeship wages were low and I needed to help my mother financially if I could. So instead I worked in the milking parlour at Home Farm for two years.

Lad Porter – 1942 to 1944

Towards the end of 1941 I applied for a lad porter job at Chippenham Railway Station, my former headmaster at Calne Senior School and Mr Forbes, Bailiff to the Marquis of Lansdowne provided references.

I started work on 26 January 1942. I was not quite 16 years old. My staff number was 97343 and service badge number was 46813. I was issued with a peak cap with GWR on the front, as it was wartime I had to wait nearly 6 months for a full uniform, which was issued to certain grades.

My hours of duty were 8 a.m. to 4 p.m. At that time there were no other lad porters employed so my duties were to sweep the platforms, making sure no debris was swept onto the line, dusting the platform seats, and a general tidy of the booking office and waiting rooms. The heating on the station was coal fires. Waiting rooms, station master's office and booking office were all heated by coal so another of my tasks was to clean the fireplaces of spent ash; light fires and replenish the coal as required, most of the time being a general dogsbody.

Once a week I had to go to Christian Malford Halt to sweep the platforms and generally tidy up, walk to the post office in the village where the tickets were issued to bring back what was called 'Returns' to the Booking office at Chippenham. Another day I would go to Stanley and Lacock Halts to again sweep and tidy up.

The joy of the job was taking notices to the East and West signal boxes. I used to stay as long as I possibly could because I was so interested in the work they did.

After a short while other lad porters were employed so this meant we had two shifts of duty 6 a.m. to 2 p.m. and 2 p.m. to 10 p.m. We sometimes were given additional jobs to do, such as when engines had

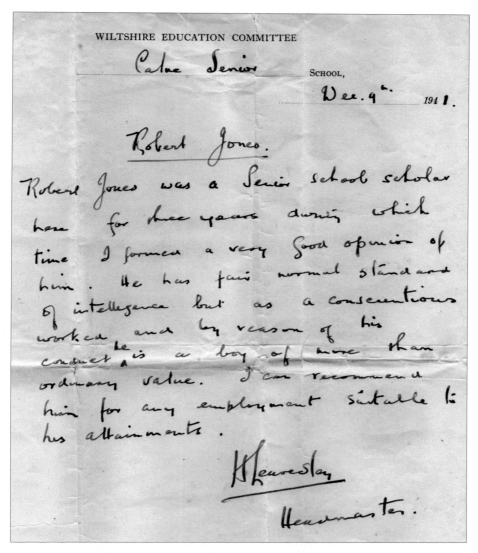

WILTSHIRE EDUCATION COMMITTEE

Calne Senior SCHOOL,

Dec. 9ᵗʰ 1941.

Robert Jones.

Robert Jones was a Senior school scholar here for three years during which time I formed a very good opinion of him. He has fair normal standard of intelligence but as a conscientious worker and by reason of his conduct he is a boy of more than ordinary value. I can recommend him for any employment suitable to his attainments.

H Heaveslay

Headmaster.

Letter of reference from Headmaster of Calne Senior School

to run round or perhaps change engines we had to uncouple or couple up. This could be quite difficult; the coupling could become tight, if this occurred we had to ask the driver to 'ease up' to loosen them a little. The operation started by first uncoupling the vacuum pipe. As soon as this was completed you knew nothing could move, as the brakes would be

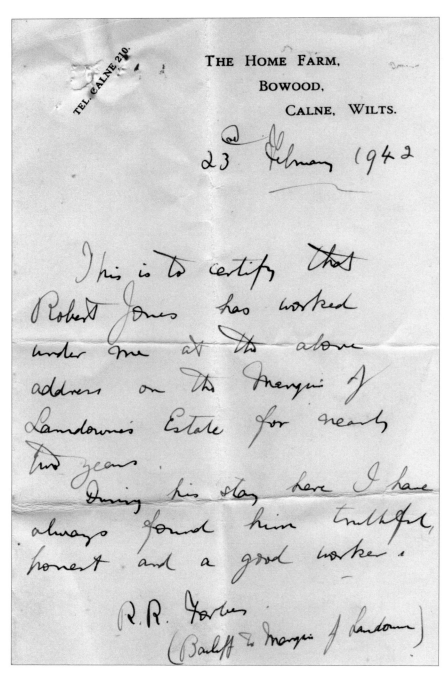

THE HOME FARM,
BOWOOD,
CALNE, WILTS.

23 February 1942

This is to certify that Robert Jones has worked under me at the above address on the Marquis of Lansdowne's Estate for nearly two years.

During his stay here I have always found him truthful, honest and a good worker.

R. R. Forbes
(Bailiff to Marquis of Lansdowne)

Letter of reference from Mr R Forbes Bailiff to the Marquis of Lansdowne

Left: GWR Cap badge

Below: The pagoda shelter at Stanley Bridge Halt which I would sweep once a week – this photograph was taken later probably in the 1960s.

fully on. The coupling could be unscrewed and lifted off the hook; the vacuum pipe was then put onto the vacuum stop on the engine.

In winter the steam pipe for heating the carriages had to be disconnected, first turning the tap to off, sometimes the tap was very hot indeed, great care was needed for safety. It was an extremely dirty job, the coupling having to be kept well oiled, though I never minded getting my hands dirty. The drivers always had a constant supply of cotton waste on the engine for hand cleaning. You rarely saw a driver without a handful of cotton waste. I was given to understand this came from the sweepings from factory floors; wherever it came from it was something not to be without. Night duty was soon introduced for us lads from 10 p.m. to 6 a.m. One night the linesman was needed to rectify a fault at Chippenham East signal box and I was detailed to find Unity Street in the blackout and awaken him, as few people had private telephones.

The stationmaster at this time was Mr. Freddie Gale a real GWR gentleman with his pillbox hat, and black bowler when off duty, always immaculate. We never thought of calling our superiors by their first names so he was always Mr. Gale. When someone asked the time of the next train to a certain place and he told the passenger the time, which could be awhile to wait perhaps, the passenger would often say 'not one before that?' He would get annoyed and immediately hit back with, 'you asked for the next train; that is the time'. Another side of him, he called us lad porters 'his little lambs', we looked up to him with respect. He lived in Marshfield Road. Tom Smith an engine driver lived in the Station Master house. After the war the house was demolished together with the stables and other buildings to make way for the car park; one building still remains which Brunel used as an office, there is a blue plague on the wall to commemorate this.

The goods department had two horse-drawn wagons to deliver goods in the town. At the end of the day the horses were released and made their own way to the stables behind the Station House, stopping on the way at the windows of the refreshment rooms where the girls would give them sugar lumps. Lorries were used for deliveries outside the town.

Some of the land owned by the Great Western Railway around the station, was suitable for cultivation and used by railwaymen as allotments.

Chippenham Station was a good place to see new engines from Swindon Works, and other engines, which had been in the works for repair or overhaul and painting. They were tested on a local stopping train to Bristol and back, some were from all parts of the Great Western Railway. Some coaches were also tested in this way.

World War 2 was being fought at this time, so only a minimum of light was allowed on the platforms. The station was all gas lighting. The globes were painted blue with a small portion left so light only shone directly downwards. There were two lights on the over-bridge from platform to platform; these were manually lit and extinguished. When air raid attacks were imminent it was known as 'Amber alert' and this was sent through to the booking office. Sometimes when it was found to be a raid nearer to Chippenham it was changed to 'Red alert'. The two bridge lights were extinguished immediately for the duration of the raid, so with dim lighting everywhere on the station it was rather dangerous for anybody moving about. The lights beyond the station canopy were never lit during wartime. All the lights were manually operated having a chain to pull for on or off and lit by a by-pass pilot flame.

Electricity did not come to Chippenham railway station until after the war had ended.

Another precaution taken at this time was to paint the edges of the platforms with a white strip this helped passengers from taking a tumble down onto the line. Unfortunately this did happen occasionally.

Fresh water was obtained from the only tap on the station, this was situated on the down platform and had to supply everyone's needs.

The Railway had an internal system for mail, which circulated all over the network. A rack of pigeon holes in the guard's van on passenger trains were set up for this purpose. Important letters had to be signed for at every transfer. On the platform were pigeon holes for the goods and other local departments.

The Swindon Railway Works closed each year for the annual works holiday; this involved putting on special trains to holiday resorts such as Weymouth, Torquay, Paignton and Penzance. During the week special coaches or reservations were put on regular trains and of course specials trains for the homeward return.

The Railway had their own telephone system throughout to departments such as Local, Goods, Stations, Signal boxes, Branches and Wayside yards. Exchanges were at principal stations and could be connected to the General Post Office - GPO telephones in special circumstances.

In North Wiltshire there were a number of Royal Air Force camps:

- Yatesbury, Compton Bassett, Lyneham, Melksham, Hullavington, Corsham and Colerne. A Royal Navy Stores was at Copenacre. Lots of goods, supplies of all sorts came into Chippenham to be transported on local trains to these camps, or by road using the loading bank outside the front of the station. I remember seeing cartons of Lyons cakes piled high on barrows with nets of Brussels sprouts ready for transportation. On occasions we young lads would run down the platform with barrows which were very full; once I recall one overloaded barrow going out of control onto the line. Great speed was needed to recover the goods before a train was due. Another incident concerning a barrow, which was stacked too high and resulted in one of the platform lights being knocked off - high spirits of youth, I guess.

Throughout this time thousands of airmen were passing through Chippenham. On night duty one of us had to travel on the 10.30 p.m. train to Swindon to assist with airmen alighting at Dauntsey. Going up towards Christian Malford on dark nights, the driver watched out for the River Avon which glimmered in the dark, he knew he must slow down as he was approaching Christian Malford Halt, his next stop which had no lights at all. We returned back to Chippenham on the 11.35 p.m. from Swindon, stopping only at Dauntsey where more airmen would alight to make their way back to Lyneham. The guard of this train was a porter-guard; he went through to Taunton via Westbury, coming back the next evening on the mainline train from Taunton to London Paddington via Bristol. This duty was called 'Double home' as he lodged one night away from home.

On the way home to Derry Hill I passed by the London Road Cemetery, on one occasion I was fortunate to listen to the nightingale singing in the copse nearby where Hardings Mead is now - a lovely reward at the end of a late shift.

Another incident, which happened by the Cemetery in London Road, when I was going home from Swindon duty after mid-night. I was stopped by a home guard and asked why I was about at that time of night, I had to produce evidence of my identity and was then allowed to continue on my way home without further hindrance.

Lad porters increased in number, I remember Bob Beer, David Chamberlain, my cousin Ken Cleverly, Ken Gough, Burt Jefferies, and John Ricketts. As it was wartime, women were taken on as porters too, but did not seem to stay very long. We all eventually moved on, only Ken Cleverly worked on the railway until retirement having moved to Lancashire.

We collected our wages from the booking office; I can't remember how much it was. It was paid out in a little round tin, about 2 inches in diameter and one and a half inches high, with our allocated number on the lid. Certainly not a great deal of money could have been put in so small a space. We took the money out and checked it, then handed the tin back for future use.

During the early part of the war there was a 10 p.m. passenger and parcel train from York to Bristol via Swindon calling at Chippenham at approximately 7.30 a.m. This train was made up of mostly London North Eastern wooden coaches and parcel vans.

Sunday evenings were very busy; stacks of bicycles had gradually accumulated over the weekend, these were on the platform by the Parcel Office - far too many to be stored in the cycle shed. These were mainly owned by airmen on weekend leave.

We had to check dates on which they were left; if over the time a surcharge then had to be paid. The airmen were very good, most having the excess ready.

Fire watching was only on Sunday nights, for a number of us meeting in the first class waiting room. Fortunately we did not suffer from the scourge of incendiary bombs. However a watch was kept; things were not left to chance.

Pigeons were sometimes sent in baskets to Chippenham and other stations. The pigeons had to be released as soon as possible. We took them outside the station for their take off, recording the time of release on a label attached to the basket which was then returned to the sender. The birds always seemed to know when they were about to be set free;

they began cooing in earnest, surprisingly noisy. There was a mass of telegraph wires outside the station, on releasing the birds we had to be extremely careful not to let them make their flight towards these wires.

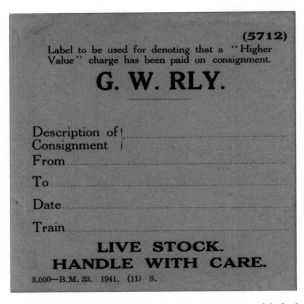

A bright red 'Live Sock Handle With Care' label
used to indentify this special type of consignment
to ensure no harm came to the animals or birds

Occasionally a coffin had to be put on or taken off a train, the undertaker or service personnel usually dealt with this. A coffin could be already on the train before it reached Chippenham and as we had to open the doors and look in all parcel vans it gave one a bit of a shock to find a coffin there instead of parcels.

I was summoned by the Government to attend a medical at Trim Street, Bath, for one of the armed services. I passed A1 and was registered for the army. I was not called to serve, as a railway employee I was classed as being in a reserved occupation.

Shunting - Thingley Junction and Beanacre 1944 - 1946

1944 brought about a change for me. At the time I was an acting grade 2 porter when a temporary position as a grade 4 shunter at Thingley Junction was offered to me on 13 January 1944. I was transferred to Thingley Junction Ministry of Defence as a shunter for Lacock and Thingley West, which had just been opened, starting on Monday 17 January 1944 on rate of pay of £2.11s (£2.55p) plus 19s.6d (97.½p war advance.

Shunters were issued with a raincoat and leggings made of a canvas like material interwoven with rubber. These were very heavy and cumbersome especially when wet. In summer heat they were even more unpleasant to wear. A sou'wester was also issued. Shunting with a pole was at first hard work becoming easier with practice. The three-link couplings were all right but screw couplings were heavy, which made them difficult to operate with a pole, especially if not oiled.

There were a number of re-enforced pillboxes around the yard, one or two were in the fields another between the down main and up branch lines. MOD policemen were stationed at different places, they mostly carried revolvers but for a while they had an issue of Sten guns. Passes had to be shown for entry into the yard. We worked with the army, the soldiers did the loading and unloading of the ammunitions mostly on No. 7 siding. Spare open wagons were stabled on No. 1 and vans on No. 10 sidings. The War Office paid part of our wages for operations such as shunting engines and the ammunition trains. All these operations were very much hush-hush, we were all sworn to secrecy.

There were some lights on poles, normally they were white but when an air raid warning was given they were changed over to blue which gave much less light. These lights were controlled from the signal box.

CIVL. SUPT'S OFFICE G.W R.
BRISTOL (TEMPLE MEAD

13th January,1944.

S1/62958/721 & 721.A.

Vacancy for temporary Class 4 Shunter - Thingley Junction. (Lacock Sidings).

It is noted temporary acting Grade 2 Porter Jones will take charge as temporary acting Class 4 Shunter,Thingley Junction (Lacock Sidings) on Monday next, the 17th instant. Rate of pay on and from that date 51/- plus 19/6d war advance.

It should be made clear to him that he is covering the vacancy for a temporary Shunter at Lacock Sidings as a temporary measure which does not constitute appointment to the service, or in the grade.

for R.G.Pole.

Mr.Williams,Thingley Jcn.
Chief Inspr.Willmott,Btol.
Inspr.Aston,Bristol.

My appointment as temporary Class 4 Shunter at Thingley Junction

A fleet of lorries with detachable trailers were going backwards and forwards to Copenacre and other entrances to the underground store. The road from Thingley to Chequers Hill had been widened where it joined the A4 to take this volume of traffic.

The road bridge between Thingley and Thingley West had been made wider with an opening for another railway line to connect the loop between these two places.

Water was pumped from a well at the bottom of the bank behind the signal box by two diesel engines, one was a reserve in case of a failure. The water was pumped into a large tank between the down main and up branch lines. This water supplied the water columns and all the yard, also there was a large water tank at Lacock which was supplied from the tank at Thingley.

Lacock water tank

One wagon examiner (commonly known as a wheel-tapper) was on duty for each shift he examined each wagon that came in and before they went into service again to make sure they were safe to run. If a wagon had a small defect a green card noting the fault was attached to the wagon but if it was serious a red card was attached for special attention, before it could be moved back into service.

Thingley West was a large signal box with a frame of 85 levers. It was mostly used for accepting the up ammunition trains and dispatching down ammunition trains from Thingley Junction, where the military dealt with the loading and unloading of these trains. Up and down loops were provided both on the up side of the main line.

There was an up and down loop from the main line to Lacock loops and sidings, this made a triangle between Thingley Junction, Thingley West and Lacock. These loops were not used very much other than to turn tender engines for ammunition trains at Thingley Junction, to save them going to Chippenham to turn on the table. We would pilot them as most drivers did not know the road on these loops. This operation was worked by telephone between the boxes with no block instruments.

Thingley West signal box

Lacock was quite a busy Ministry of Defence yard, moving coal for the Bristol Aeroplane Company. There was an enclosed compound used for Royal Naval stores where ammunitions were handled. This signal box had a frame of 67 levers. The yard had three long sidings, two reception roads and up and down loops, all on the up side of the main line.

A while after I had been at Thingley, I passed the rules at Bristol Temple Meads to be a goods guard to run trips to and from Farleigh Down, Beanacre, and Corsham, Farleigh Down was between Box and Bathampton on the downside off the main line. Being a goods guard you had to pass 'rules' set out for this job - you would be in charge of the train having to count all the wagons making sure they were in order and that all were coupled together, doors closed and sheets fastened down securely on open wagons. The usual length of a train was 60 wagons.

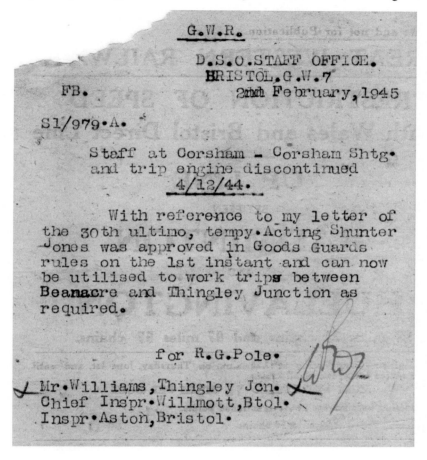

G.W.R.

D.S.O.STAFF OFFICE.
BRISTOL.G.W.7
FB.   2nd February,1945

S1/979.A.

Staff at Corsham - Corsham Shtg.
and trip engine discontinued
4/12/44.

With reference to my letter of
the 30th ultimo, tempy.Acting Shunter
Jones was approved in Goods Guards
rules on the 1st instant and can now
be utilised to work trips between
Beanacre and Thingley Junction as
required.

for R.G.Pole.

Mr.Williams,Thingley Jcn.
Chief Inspr.Willmott,Btol.
Inspr.Aston,Bristol.

Qualified in Goods Guard Rules 1 February 1945

A train journal had to be made out recording the driver's name and the weather conditions; the driver was told of the number of wagons and where these were to be detached or a pick up made.

A check had to be made that the tail lamp was on the rear of the brake van, also side lamps showing white lights forward, red to the rear. The tail lamp was most important as it is the only indication that the train is complete to a watching signalman when passing a signal box. If a goods train with vacuum fitted wagons broke away it would stop at once, but with loose couplings this would not happen. The first part attached to the engine would go on but the rest could stop in the section. If this happened the guard must go back not less than three quarters of a mile, exhibiting a hand danger signal to stop any train approaching on the obstructed line unless he arrives at a signal box within that distance. He must place detonators upon one rail of the obstructed line as follows: -

1 Detonator ¼ mile from his train
1 Detonator ½ mile from his train
3 Detonators 10 yards apart, not less than ¾ mile from his train

These instructions would also be carried out for a train failure, accident, obstruction, or other exceptional causes.

The lamps on the rear of the brake van of a goods train is a red light for the tail lamp and a side lamp on each side of the van with red lights showing to the rear and white lights showing forward. When entering a running loop the red light nearest the main line is obscured by a blank shade, which is kept in a slot on the side of the lamp for this purpose. The guard on entering the loop also has to give a signalman a hand signal to indicate that the train is complete and clear of the main line. When the train joins the main line again the guard removes the blank shade and places it back in the slot. The lamp now shows a red light to the rear.

In February 1945 I was transferred to Beanacre as a temporary class 3 shunter.

Beanacre signal box had a frame of 21 levers, this signal box was situated between Lacock and Melksham. Here we were dealing with wagons containing 500lb bombs, with one main siding for loading and unloading with a loop to run into from the down main line to the upside. Sometimes we had to leave a string of wagons on the up line while we shunted in the yard.

On one occasion it was noticed that the up main signals were clear

- the signalwoman in the box had forgotten the wagons which we had placed on the up main line. This was rectified as soon as possible and no harm was done, but it could have been serious.

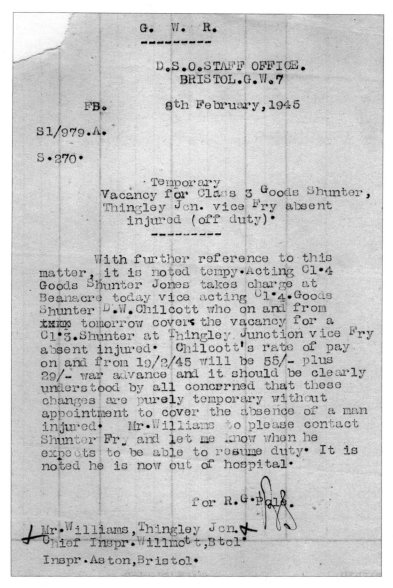

My appointment as temporary class 3 Shunter at Beanacre
8 February 1945

At Corsham we went from the down main across to the siding on the upside towards the tunnel mouth, which was nearly ¾ of a mile long. A ground frame with 2 levers was about halfway down the siding where the engine was uncoupled. Wagons which may have been pushed out from the Ministry of Defence underground opening next to Box Tunnel for dispatch were coupled to the engine. We then had to walk round the wagons to count and examine to see that sheet ties were made secure, and that brakes were off in order to travel. We then had to ask the signalman at Corsham to release the 'Annetts key' at the ground frame to unlock the point lever to proceed onto the up main then onto the brake van. When all the wagons had cleared the points they were returned to normal and the other lever being a signal, which would be left in the off' position when points were normal. The wagons would then proceed on the main line onto the brake van. The train would then be ready for Thingley.

Farleigh Down signal box had a frame of 35 levers; it was on the upside of the main line the shunting yard was on the down side of the main line. The wagons would have been marshalled in alphabetical order at Thingley for unloading in the right location. This was as instructed by the Ministry of Defence. The ammunitions after being unloaded were conveyed to the MOD underground by conveyer belts; this also applied to the ammunitions to be loaded coming out the same way. After running round and shunting in position, wagons would attached to take back to Thingley. We use to try to wait for the Box signalman to be able to clear the up 'distant' signal so the driver had a good run to get through the tunnel without struggling, the gradient being 1 in 100.

Wartime at Thingley was a place of constant activity and hustling about. There were 10 sidings, some approximately a half mile long so a shunting wagon was put to use, this being a flat wagon with running boards each side for the shunter to ride on and had rails to hold onto. The shunting wagon was always next to the shunting engine, and it also carried the re-railing ramps for re-railing a wagon if one came off the road. If it was not of a serious nature, we would be able to re-rail it ourselves; otherwise a breakdown crew would be sent from Swindon to sort the mishap. On one occasion in September 1944 I was the main cause of a derailment at the Thingley Yard, as I had not braked the vehicles shunted on the road and received a written memo saying this must be done in future.

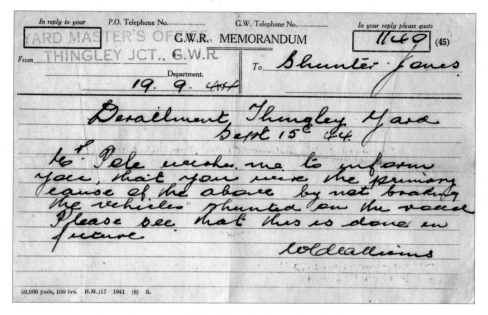

Derailment at Thingley Yard 15 September 1944

On occasions we had so many wagons in the yard that trains had to be blocked back and stabled at Thingley West and often, even as far back as Bristol and beyond to wait for us to get some dispatched to make room for these to move in. During shunting in the yard one day, I remember an incident of some 500lb bombs falling through the wagon floorboards which had broken apart! The military speedily arrived to pick them up. Thankfully these did not fall on the main line while being dispatched to their destination, which would have been a major problem or even a disaster. I'm sure we did not realise how dangerous it was working alongside these lethal weapons, especially when air raids were happening. We just got on with the job.

Learning 'First Aid' was voluntary; I began taking lessons at Chippenham run by the St. Johns' Ambulance Association, eventually going in for competitions at Bristol and Weston-Super-Mare as part of a team. These competitions were designed to be very real, with the casualties made up with fake injuries, very realistic indeed. We did come first once and several times second and third. Some of the knowledge gained I have had need to put into action a few times in cases of accident and sudden illness.

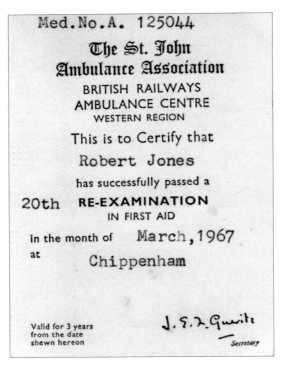

Med.No.A. 125044

The St. John Ambulance Association

BRITISH RAILWAYS
AMBULANCE CENTRE
WESTERN REGION

This is to Certify that

Robert Jones

has successfully passed a

20th RE-EXAMINATION
IN FIRST AID

in the month of   March, 1967

at   Chippenham

Valid for 3 years
from the date
shewn hereon

J. S. R. Gwilt

Secretary

My 20th Re-examination in First Aid with The St John Ambulance

If there was any spare time, which we did have from time to time, I would be in the Thingley Junction signal box (unofficially of course). It was modern in comparison to most signal boxes in the area, having an illuminated diagram with a frame of 52 levers. One sad occasion early in 1946 when a wagon examiner was in the box the signalman on duty Mr Hector Freeth collapsed, I was called to take over the box, as he was unconscious. An engine and coach was summoned from Chippenham to take him to hospital; unfortunately he died the next day, he was only aged 44. The signalman at Thingley West was told by control to switch out his box and come and take over Thingley Junction. He was qualified to take over as he relieved on Sundays. I kept the trains running until he arrived. Nothing was said to me for taking over in this emergency.

When I reached the age of 20 in February 1946 I was said to be of adult age and my wages increased to £3.1s.6d. (£3.7½p) plus £1.8s.0d (£1.40p) war advance.

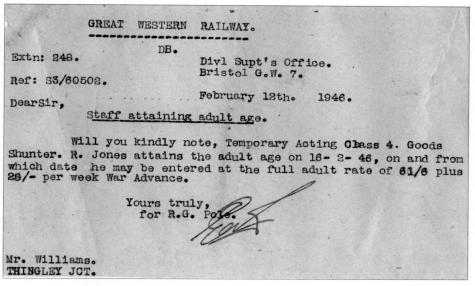

GREAT   WESTERN   RAILWAY.

                    DB.
Extn: 248.   Divl Supt's Office.
                                Bristol G.W. 7.
Ref: S3/60502.

DearSir,   February 12th.   1946.
        Staff attaining adult age.

        Will you kindly note, Temporary Acting Class 4. Goods
Shunter. R. Jones attains the adult age on 16- 2- 46, on and from
which date he may be entered at the full adult rate of 61/6 plus
28/- per week War Advance.

                    Yours truly,
                    for R.G. Pole.

Mr. Williams.
THINGLEY JCT.

Memo advising that as I had attained the of 20 I was being moved up to adult wages

Corsham Signal box
1946 – 1948

When the war ended, the system seemed to slacken off, so thinking things through I decided to apply as temporary signalman class 4 at Corsham. I was accepted, and commenced learning the workings of this signal box which had 39 levers, on 7 May 1946, taking over on Tuesday 11 June 1946 with an increased wage of £3.5.6d (£3.27½p) plus £1.8s.0d (£1.40p) war advance total of £4.13s.6d (£4.67½p).

G. W. R.

Divl. Supt's Office
BRISTOL T.M.

S1/1215.B.   7th June, 1946.

Vacancy for Temporary Goods Shunter, Thingley Junction
vice Jones.

With further reference to this matter, Jones came to this Office today and was approved as a Class 4 Signalman, Corsham Box, and will take charge on Tuesday June 11th, on and from which date he can be paid at the rate of 65/6 and 28/- per week War Advance, on and from the same date Class 4 Signalman Slade will remove to Thingley Junction to commence learning Class 5 Signalman's duties.

Please let me know when Slade is ready to come to this Office before taking charge.

for R.G.Pole.

Mr.Williams, Thingley Junction.
Mr.Boundy, Corsham.
Inspr. Aston, Bristol.
Chief Inspr. Willmott, Bristol.

My appointment as temporary Class 4 Signalman at Corsham signal box

I thought I would be very nervous when the responsibility was all mine, so I bought a packet of cigarettes, but never smoked them.

G. W. R.

Divl.Supt's Office,
BRISTOL T.M.

7th May, 1946.

Ref:- S1/1215.B.

Vacancy for Temporary Goods Shunter,
Thingley Junction vice Jones.

In connection with the above Temporary
Acting Grade 2 Porter Sutton takes charge as
Temporary Acting Class 4 Goods Shunter, Thingley
Junction today, 7/5/46; rate of pay 61/6d plus
22/6d per week War Advance.

He should clearly understand that he is
covering the vacancy for a Temporary Shunter at
Thingley purely as an emergency measure which in no
way constitutes appointment to the service or in
the grade.

Temporary Class 4 Goods Shunter Jones
removes to Corsham Signal Box today to commence
learning Temporary Class 4 Signalman's duties. He
will retain his present rate of pay while learning;
please advise me when he is ready to come here for
approval in the rules.

for R.G. Pole.

Mr.Boundy, Corsham.
Mr.Williams, Thingley Jct.
Chief Insp.Willmott, Bristol.
Insp.Aston, Bristol.

*Approval to learn duties as temporary Class 4 Signalman at
Corsham signal box 7 May 1946*

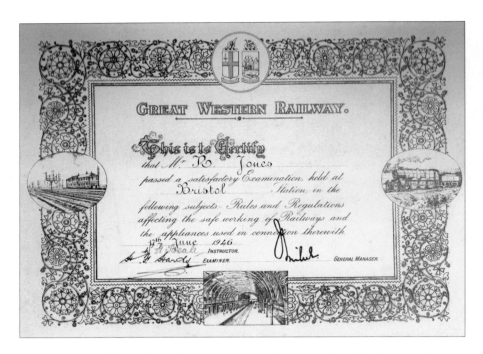

My certificate dated 17 June 1946 showing that I had passed an examination in Rules and Regulations affecting the safe working of Railways and the appliances used in connection therewith

No smoking carriage sign

Above: Corsham signal box

Right: Corsham signal box – signalling diagram

Below: Pulling a level in Corsham signal box

Left and below: Corsham signal box interior showing levers and block shelf above

Below: Corsham signal box – upper arm is down main starting signal No. 4. The lower arm is down main to up siding starting signal No. 7, this used to lead to a mysterious siding under Box Hill

To be able to apply for the post at Corsham on a permanent basis I first needed to be accepted for a class 5 signalman position. It was probably March 1947 when a vacancy at Ogbourne near Marlborough was posted on the list of signal box vacancies in the Bristol area. I applied and was selected to go to Ogbourne. My present job at Corsham signal box was then posted; I was then able to apply for Corsham as a permanent post, which thankfully I was given. I was so pleased not to have to take up the position at Ogbourne.

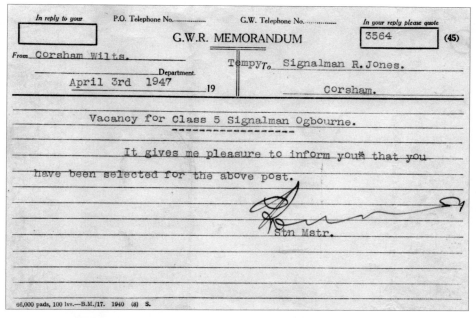

My appointed as Class 5 Signalman at Ogbourne signal box

A signalman had many regulations and rules to learn, including observing every train as it passed the box to see that all doors were closed or if anything appeared wrong with the train. On goods trains especially looking at the axle boxes which sometimes ran hot and smoke appeared and occasionally caught fire - this was called a 'hot box'. The ones that were lubricated with oil were not often affected, however some of the older wagons used grease for lubrication - these were most likely to 'run hot' and would sometimes catch fire. The most important thing to watch for was the tail lamp as this was an indication that the train was complete, especially with loose couplings on goods trains.

Train passing Corsham signal box

There were many other regulations to observe. When it became foggy we had to call fogmen to go to certain signals such as 'distant' and some stop signals. They would place detonators on the line; for a 'distant' signal, 1 detonator if it was in the caution position and give a yellow hand signal to the driver. For a stop signal it would be 3 detonators on the line and a red hand signal to the driver. These hand signals would be by flags in daylight and a hand lamp in darkness. The fogman would be sent for when visibility was less than 200 yards; this was usually determined by not being able to see a certain signal from the box, or the back light of a signal or some other point. In some signal boxes greatcoats with red collars were kept for the fogmen to use in adverse conditions. At some places a fogman would be outside the signal box to watch for the tail lamps of passing trains and report to the signalman. Fogmen were mostly from the Permanent Way department and could be called at anytime of the day or night, having to sign on and off duty in the train register book. At some stop signals there was a lever which when pulled placed 3 detonators on the line. Small huts were supplied for the fogmen to shelter in to have some protection from the weather and some warmth from a brazier.

Winter weather brought its hazards; heavy snow would tend to prevent the movement of points and the Permanent Way department needed to be summoned to keep the points clear. In the meantime we reversed the points as frequently as we could, doing our best to keep them clear.

Once we had a message to say that the smoke box on the front of the engine was glowing with red-hot ash; as it was dark it showed up as a red headlamp. I think the train proceeded to Bristol to change the engine.

At Corsham signal box Box Tunnel regulations had to be learnt. There was also what was called a single needle instrument, this being a pointer going left to right with different tones, (as the Morse code has dots and dashes). This was one of the few instruments left of its kind, others being at Bristol Office, Chippenham Booking Office, Box, Holt Junction and Melksham signal boxes. I never completely learnt all the codes but knew when Corsham was being called. I then rang Bristol by telephone for whatever message I needed to receive. A lot of words were in the code. Just before 11 a.m. every morning the time signal was sent on the single needle instrument from Bristol. This began with a slow left, right, left movement, then a pause with the needle held over to the left, until 11 a.m. when a rapid left to right movement took place, this then was the 'time check' the bell code 8-5-5 was then sent on the block bells, this going to other signal boxes in the area which did not have the needle. The single needle instrument was removed shortly after I took over at Corsham, the time check being sent on the block bells only. Clocks were checked and recorded in the train register, if it was slow, fast or correct time.

Colours played a very important part in a signal box; signal box levers were painted different colours for the operation they performed.

Red	Stop signals including ground shunt signals
Yellow	Distant signals
Black	Points
Blue	Facing point locks
Part Blue/Brown	Electrical release for ground frame etc.
Black with White	Chevrons pointed down for detonators on down road, up for detonators on up road
White	Spare
Short handles	For signals & points electrically worked

At Box some of the up goods trains needed a banker engine coupled to the guards van at the rear to assist up through Box Tunnel, because of the rising gradient through the tunnel being 1 in 100. This would mean stopping at Box to couple and Corsham to uncouple, but most times trains went by Box and the banker was sent on to assist after the train passed. The guard would take the tail lamp off and not put it on until he was able to show it to the signalman at Corsham, who would not send 'Train out of section' bell code 2-1 to Box until the banker had arrived. The bell code for engine assisting in the rear was 2-2, sent after Corsham had acknowledged 2 bells to confirm 'Train entering section'. Once I remember the banker was sent from Box after the train went by, but never caught the train up, so was not needed to assist that time.

Some Bath stone was still loaded at Box and Corsham. These blocks of stone were of various sizes from huge to more manageable pieces. A cloud of dust would arise when sawing was taking place as stones were prepared for transit.

Coal also was unloaded in the sidings at Corsham, on the station side of the signal box; this business belonged to Mr. Hancock the Coal

Merchant. He owned a very old lorry with block tyres which moved the coal around in the yard. This type of lorry was the last of its kind I have seen in working order.

A Scammell mechanical horse was also used to at Corsham to lift and transport goods.

Scammell mechanical horse with Corsham signal box in background

As mentioned earlier the gradient through Box Tunnel is 1 in 100 rising towards Corsham. Wire 5 feet from the ground was fixed to the wall through the tunnel on the up side, if a train stopped, not able to make the gradient, the guard would cut the wire; this would ring a bell in Box and Corsham signal boxes, or Thingley Junction when Corsham was switched out. A lot of special regulations were in force for the tunnel, for example warning down trains that a train was stopped on the up main line. Also there were three telephones one at each end of the tunnel and one in the middle. These were tested every day by the ganger, this being written in the train register as all messages had to be recorded.

On a good day I could stand outside Corsham signal box and see an up stopping train in Box Mill Lane Halt, the tunnel was so straight. Most of the time the tunnel was filled with smoke despite having several air vents throughout its length.

Travelling to Corsham was 8 miles from my home in Derry Hill, so my BSA C11 motorcycle which I bought from Ventnor of Melksham in May 1947 made the journey to work less arduous. The Permanent Way Gang made a lean-to for me to keep it dry. It was a surprise - I had no idea they had this in mind to do; how grateful I was!

Arthur Smith the shunter there in his spare moments would file and fashion a piece of oak to a corkscrew shape that eventually became a table lamp. I am the proud owner of two of them.

Going home on my motorcycle was not without incident: I came over the railway bridge near the Roebuck Inn (now a private dwelling house) and skidded on some wet leaves. I just went over and stepped off the bike, unfortunately the bike went on and hit the headlamp against a gatepost damaging the coil ignition switch, and it could not be started again. I had to push the motorcycle to Lacock garage where they made a temporary repair. I had to send the ignition switch to Lucas and wait several weeks for it to be repaired and sent back to me. In the meantime I had to use a pushbike again which put hard work back into my travelling. Thankfully I was never late for duty.

Once while waiting for a local goods train Chippenham to Bathampton to clear Box signal box, a stopping passenger train Chippenham to Bristol had stopped outside the signal box. The driver asked me if I would like a cup of tea, so I took my cup to him to be filled. When the goods train cleared Box I obtained line clear so I lowered the signal for the passenger train to proceed, it was only stopped for a few seconds. Any passengers watching may have thought he had only stopped to give me a cup of tea!

The Nationalisation of the Railways was 1 January 1948. Detonators were exploded on the up main line by an engine between Chippenham West and Chippenham East. I heard them over the phone in my signal box at Corsham.

Box Tunnel

The building of the tunnel began in 1836 with trial shafts most of the shafts 70 to 300ft. In 1838 the construction work was let to contractors George Burge of Herne Bay working form the western end and locally based Lewis and Brewer working from the eastern end. Excavation from the western end was done with picks and shovels and was lined with brickwork, while excavation at the eastern end was blasted out and left unlined with bare rock for roof and sides. Work went on night and day.1100 to 1200 men and more than 100 horses employed. During the last six months this was increased to 4000 men and 300 horses. Nearly 100 men are said to have been killed during the 5 years it took to complete the tunnel. A lot of the work was hindered by water, the incline is 1 in 100 falling to the west about 1¾ miles long. 247,000 cubic yards of earth and stone was excavated. Thirty million bricks were used in all, and weekly a ton of gunpowder and a ton of candles for lighting.

Block telegraph was installed through the tunnel December 1847. When clear of smoke it is said that in early April (particularly 9 April Brunel's birthday) the rising sun can be seen from the west end through the tunnel.

A friend and I walked right through Box Tunnel and back again one Sunday morning when Corsham box was switched out. It is 3212 yards (approximately 1¾ miles) long. Corsham up main 'distant' signal was 1547 yards from the signal box (about ¼ mile into the tunnel). It had only yellow and green shades as an arm would not have been visible. My friend took a photograph - I wonder if this was the only one ever taken of this signal. The lampman never trimmed this lamp, it was always done by a member of the Permanent Way Gang.

Corsham up main distant signal No. 37 was 1547 yards from the box about ¼ mile from the exit of the tunnel and had only yellow and green shades

My BSA motorcycle which I bought in May 1947

Chippenham West Signal box 1948 – 1951

Moving again, this time to Chippenham West signal box a class 3 box; taking over on 11 October 1948, this was nearer home and much less travelling for me.

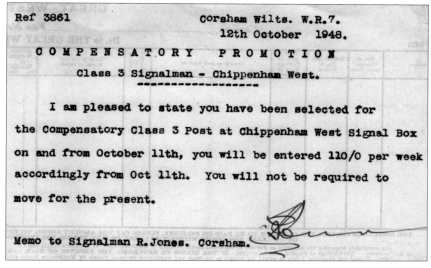

Ref 3861   Corsham Wilts. W.R.7.
                       12th October 1948.

C O M P E N S A T O R Y   P R O M O T I O N

      Class 3 Signalman - Chippenham West.

    I am pleased to state you have been selected for the Compensatory Class 3 Post at Chippenham West Signal Box on and from October 11th, you will be entered 110/0 per week accordingly from Oct 11th. You will not be required to move for the present.

Memo to Signalman R. Jones. Corsham.

Above: Appointment as Class 3 signalman at Chippenham West signal box with a wage of 110 shillings (£5.50).

Left: Chippenham West signal box

Chippenham West signal box – looking east towards the station

Right: Chippenham West signal box interior showing levers and various indicating equipment on shelf above

Left: Chippenham West signal box looking west. Signals from left to right: down main home signal No. 25; down bay home, signal No. 24; down bay (Weymouth bay) to siding signal No. 22; and up main backing to down main siding signal No. 13 indicating equipment above

Above: Chippenham West signal box interior showing levers

Right: Engine No. 6997 at Chippenham West signal box.

Above and right: Looking west from Chippenham West signal box, note West box inner home signal No. 3, Chippenham East signal box – up main distant signal No. 63 behind diesel train

Left: Chippenham West signal box – inner home signal No. 3; also note driver stops for number of carriages on down trains

Chippenham West signal box – up inner home signal No. 3, Chippenham East signal box – up main distant signal No. 63 when West signal box switch out not in use

Chippenham West signal box – up main distant No. 1.

It had a 27-lever frame; nevertheless it was quite busy at times with a lot of extra bell codes, as it was a short section to Chippenham East signal box. It had to deal with engines running round trains and vehicles being attached and detached. Number 2 platform was called the 'Weymouth Bay' and it was only possible to shunt into and out at the west end. Another siding was on the town bridge between the up and down main lines; in addition there was a short siding off the up main. This was called the 'Horse Box' siding; but no horses were loaded there in my working life.

Sometimes the engines of down passenger trains stopped outside the signal box and if it blew off steam as sometimes happened - I could not hear anything at all. I would have to stand right up to the bells to hear if they rang. There was not much regulating to do; I was mainly concerned with activity at 'Weymouth Bay' as most regulating was done at Thingley or Chippenham East signal boxes. Another thing we did was for passenger trains, we asked 1 pause 3 and freight trains 1 pause 2 bell code if they were for the branch to the Westbury and Weymouth line.

The GPO Sorting Office was next to Chippenham Station with a back entrance onto the platform where mail was transferred on and off most trains.

There was apparatus for mail exchange situated on the down main line near Lowden Bridge 600 yards further down the line from the station it was designed for receiving and dispatching mailbags. The postmen would telephone the Chippenham West signal box at about 11.30 p.m. to say that they were in position, waiting in the hut provided.

The Travelling Post Office train would have been signalled from signal box to signal box as all trains are. The TPO 10.20 p.m. from Paddington to Bristol was due through Chippenham around midnight each night, when the bell code 4 bells was received at Chippenham West signal box it would be passing Dauntsey a few miles up the line. The signalman would telephone the postmen that the train was approaching and they would proceed to fix up the mailbags for exchange. These bags were made with very strong material.

As the train passed Chippenham West signal box the sliding doors of the train would already be open for this routine to begin. The mailbags to be picked up were positioned on the apparatus designed for receiving and dispatching mail bags. The mail dispatched by the postmen on the train was caught in a net on the apparatus. All this happened while the train was travelling at full speed. The manoeuvres worked perfectly for years, continuing even during the war years and for sometime afterwards.

The instructions for the Travelling Post Office staff were:

CHIPPENHAM (exchange location) 600 yards west of station
Three miles west of Dauntsey observe viaduct
Notice sideline, Signal cabin with level crossing, on passing through Chippenham Station and over long stone viaduct, at a white board, lower and extend the apparatus on the side of the train.

No apparatus was provided for the up direction at Chippenham East.

Chippenham East Signal box
1951 – 1955

Another move came for me when one of the signalmen Ted Allen at Chippenham East signal box developed a condition with his legs, which made it impossible for him to pull the heavy levers. It was agreed for me to work Chippenham East signal box as a temporary measure in exchange to see if his health improved. I started there on 10 October 1951. I have been given to understand that I was the youngest signalman to work East Box, I was twenty-five.

Chippenham East signal box

It was the most interesting box for me, much larger than any that I had worked before. It had 64 levers, though the highest number was 63, as there was a zero at the other end of the frame. (This was unusual as it had been added on the end of the frame.) It controlled the down 'distant' which was motor operated, so the lever had its handle shortened by six inches as it only worked an electric switch. Bath Station also had a zero lever for the same reason as Chippenham East signal box.

Chippenham East signal box interior – levers and block shelf above,
I bought the wall clock from British Rail when the signal box closed

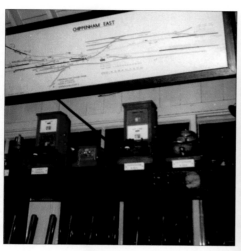

Chippenham East signal box interior – signalling diagram and block shelf below

Above: Electronic token for the Calne Branch Line being handed to me by the driver

Above and right: Chippenham East signal box – junction with Calne branch line from left to right branch home signal No. 4 and down main signal No.2

Left: Chippenham East signal box – up main advance starting signal No. 56, Langley Crossing signal box – up main distant signal No. 4

Below: Chippenham East signal box down main home signal No. 1

Left: Chippenham East signal box – up branch fixed distant signal, Calne branch line – looking towards Chippenham; note gasometer in the distance. In my day fixed distant signals did not have numbers, everything has a number now

Right and below: Chippenham East signal box – branch home signal No. 3 and the 5.35 p.m. Calne to Chippenham diesel train on 18 September 1965

The station master would visit signal boxes almost every day to sign the Train Register especially if the box was near the station, not so often if further away. The register was also signed by any official visiting the box. Chippenham East signal box did not carry out the full booking; it was what was called a 'skeleton booking'. All Calne trains were recorded and other trains which were delayed. Also recorded were box to box messages, signing on and off duty and any other important messages. Most other boxes recorded everything. Some of the busier boxes would have a booking boy to do this.

The signal inspector would sometimes call and sign the register, and he would occasionally ask us some rules. Once a year at least he would test us on the rules very thoroughly. If when he came he had a relief signalman with him we knew we were in for a gruelling. Sometimes he took us outside while the relief took over our duty. We usually knew the inspector was on the way through the grapevine. Inspectors were all very nice to get on with as most had been signalmen themselves.

At Chippenham East and West signal boxes the 'distant' signals between the two boxes were lower arms of the stop signals of the box in rear and were not out the required distance to accept trains under regulation 4, so regulation 4A 'Line clear to clearing point', acceptance bell code 2-2-2 was used. At East signal box if 'Line clear' had not been received from Langley Crossing 2-2-2 would be given to West signal box; which when acknowledged East signal box would place the block indicator to 'Line clear'. West signal box would maintain its 'distant' signal at caution. Similarly, West signal box, if it did not have 'Line clear' from Thingley Junction would give 2-2-2 to East signal box who would acknowledge; West signal box would then place the block indicator to 'Line clear' and East signal box would then maintain its 'distant' signals at caution. If either signal box received 'Line clear' from the signal box ahead before receiving 'Train entering section', then the appropriate 'distant' signal would be lowered. This meant that East signal box had the line clear through to Thingley Junction, and West signal box had the line clear through to Langley Crossing before the 'distant' signals could be lowered.

There were a lot of special bell codes used between these two boxes, such as for engines running round and wrong road working.

One frosty morning I had what was called a 'Wrong side failure'. When the 5.30 a.m. Paddington was between the down main 'home' signal and down main 'inner home' signal it did not operate the track indicator in the box; it showed 'Track clear' when it should have shown 'Track occupied'. The Lineman was called and changed the relay immediately and took it to Swindon Signal Department on the next train, but before he arrived at Swindon the contacts came free, so it was suggested that somehow moisture had entered and frozen the mechanism.

The yard was very busy sometimes with a 'Pilot engine' on up and down side; also the local shed with engines going in and out. Some of the trains which terminated at Chippenham had tender engines; these needed to turn, as did engines for ammunition trains at Thingley. The turntable was full size so was able to turn any engine as required.

At Chippenham East, Thingley Junction and some other boxes where there was a shunting yard a megaphone was issued. This was used to call the shunter or other members of staff with a message, if they were not in a natural calling distance, or if there was a good deal of noise in the goods yard. The megaphone was a simple old-fashioned piece of equipment but very useful; it was made of metal a cone about 2 feet long tapering from approximately 1 foot to 2 inches diameter.

Freight trains had to be regulated, especially when they had traffic 'off' or 'on'. Control always advised us how many wagons were on a train, as the down refuge would hold only 50 wagons. Where the normal load was 60 wagons, we sometimes crossed a freight train onto the Calne Branch provided there was no train accepted from Calne at this time.

Calne services were mostly run by push-pull auto trains, but other trains had to be run round between East and West signal boxes which involved the up and down lines. Sometimes this was difficult to fit in with the main line trains. A lot of special bell codes were used for these operations. The Calne Branch was a single line worked by electric token; only one token could be out of the machine at any one time. The plunger on the machine operated a bell and needle at each end of the section. Call attention was one beat. Calne signal box would answer with one beat. Chippenham East signal box would ask for the auto train 3-1-3. Calne signal box would give back 3-1-3 and hold his plunger in; this would hold the needle over; East box signalman would then be able to withdraw the token by turning it in the machine; the bell would ring at both ends and the Calne box signalman would know that the token had been taken out at East signal box. When the train left East signal box the signalman would give 2 beats 'Train entering section'; Calne signal box would give back 2 beats. When the train arrived at Calne and the driver handed the token to the signalman, he would place it in the machine and give 2-1 'Train out of section' to East signal box who would acknowledge by giving 2-1. When Calne required the train to return to Chippenham, the operation would be repeated in reverse.

Chippenham to Calne was a pleasant and lovely 6 mile journey especially going through Hazeland wood. All the way along the side of the track was a water pipe which supplied water to the Harris Bacon factory from Langley Burrell where I presume there was a reservoir, small lengths of pipe can still be seen along the side of the present cycle track. There were wires on the telephone poles to the factory to indicate the level of the water at Langley. If the water level should fall below a certain level a bell would ring at the factory. What action was taken if this incident arose I am not sure.

There was a lot of lever movement in East signal box; No. 46 point from the down platform to the down sidings was I think near the limit for a 'manual point' from a signal box, though it was reasonable as it was in constant use. A point much nearer could be just as hard having less usage; you got to know how much weight to put behind each lever.

Shunting at East End of Down Platform

In order to avoid the necessity of verbally advising the signalman of certain operations required to be carried out, a block bell was provided in Chippenham East signal box connected to one in a small case at the London end of the down platform. When necessary the following bell signals would be sent to the signalman by the foreman or person conducting the shunting operations.

Description	Number of Beats to be given
Call Attention	1
Close Points	2
Train or Vehicles on Down Line for Down Sidings	3
Train or Vehicles on Down Sidings for Down main Line	1 pause 2
Train or Vehicles on Down Line for Spur	4
Train or Vehicles in Spur for Down Line	2 pause 2
Engine or Vehicles from Spur to Bay or Vice Versa	3 pause 1
Close Spur Catch Point	1 pause 3
Engine or vehicles from Spur to Bay Siding or Vice Versa	3 pause 3
Engine or Vehicles to cross from Down Line to Up Line	5
Engine or Vehicles required to propel up the Down Line	2 pause 5
Obstruction Danger	6

The following special instructions applied:

The words 'Engine and Vehicles' must be understood to refer only to a light engine or engine with vehicles not containing passengers.

The 'Call Attention' signal must precede all other signals except 'Obstruction Danger'.

The bell signals must be sent slowly and distinctly to the signalman and if the required movement can be made they must be repeated by him. Until they are correctly returned, the station staff must clearly understand that the movement cannot be made. If the signals are not correctly returned they must again be sent.

Shunting operations must be performed with care. Where movements of engines and wagons have to be made in certain circumstances some distance from the signal box the signalman and others must be perfectly clear with each other as to what movement is required to be carried out. Shunters and others in charge of the shunting operations must see that the points are properly worked in response to the bell signals before the shunting is commenced and that they are set for the main line when work is completed.

Friday market days were interesting. In early evening the drovers would drive the cattle from the market which was held in the centre of Chippenham, what is now the Borough Parade. From the market site the animals were driven through the town up Monkton Hill to the cattle pens, which were opposite East signal box to be loaded into cattle wagons.

The siding next to the Calne Bay No.4 platform was called 'New Found Out'; I was intrigued to hear of different names given to sidings such as The Lay-by, The Shute, Milk Siding and School Siding.

The usual shift working in signal boxes was early shift 6 a.m. to 2 p.m., late shift 2 p.m. to 10 p.m. and night shift 10 p.m. to 6 a.m. If someone was off sick or on leave a relief man would cover the duty. Sometimes this was not possible, so the two regular signalmen would divide the duty hours doing 6 a.m. to 6 p.m. or 6 p.m. to 6 a.m. to cover. After a week of 12 hour shifts we were rather tired.

It was during my time working at this box that I got married first living in rooms in Ivy Road, Chippenham and a year later buying a new build bungalow in Cricketts Lane. As I had not been in military service during the war it was difficult to get a council house, so Margaret and I decided to apply for a mortgage which was eventually successful.

My wife and I working in garden of our new home in Cricketts Lane

The signalman who I had exchanged with recovered his health and I returned to Chippenham West signal box on 20 April 1955. Chippenham East signal box had been most interesting and I was very happy there.

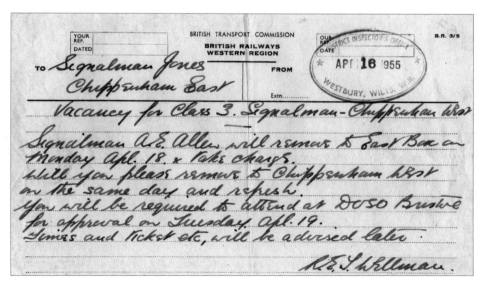

Order to return to Chippenham West signal box

Thingley Junction Signal box
1955 – 1957

A vacancy occurred at Thingley Junction signal box; I applied and was transferred, taking over on 7 December 1955.

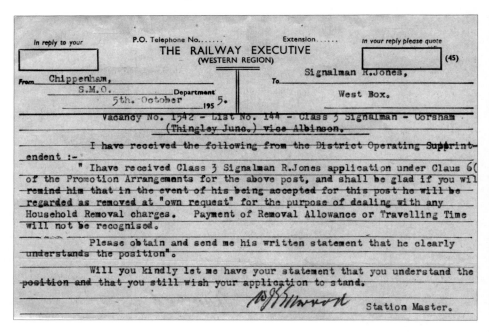

Memo in response to application for vacancy at Thingley Junction signal box

This box held my interest; I did not find it difficult to learn as I had spent so much of my spare time there while shunting in the yard a few years earlier; Thingley Junction signal box had 52 levers and an illuminated diagram for track circuits throughout between all of the signals. It was a busy box, although as it was no longer wartime not quite so busy as before, but we still had a number of ammunition trains to deal with. Thingley West signal box had closed but was not taken out and Lacock was still a working signal box. There was a lot of regulating of trains, to fit in with main line and branch line services.

Thingley Junction signal box

Thingley Junction signal box – signalling diagram

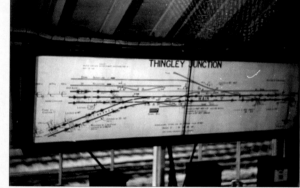

Thingley Junction signal box interior showing leavers and block shelve above

Thingley Junction signal box interior showing leavers and block shelve above

Right: Thingley Junction signal box – signalling mechanism on ground floor

Below: The Flying Scotsman passing Thingley signal box

Diesel train at Thingley signal box

Above and opposite: Views around Thingley Junction looking towards Chippenham

*Thingley Junction –
looking towards the
junction and water
tower*

Thingley Junction signal box – up main distant signal No. 1

Thingley Junction signal box – up branch home signal No. 4 installed probably about 1938

Thingley Junction signal box – up main advance starting signal No. 9

Thingley Junction signal box – down main intermediate home signal No. 50 and disc to up and down loop or up sidings, looking towards Corsham

Thingley Junction signal box – down main distant signal No. 52, looking towards Chippenham

Left: Thingley Junction signal box – down main distant signal No. 52, looking towards Thingley Junction

Below: Thingley Junction signal box – colour light down main distant No. 52, which replaced the semaphore signal in the early 1960s and was located some distance nearer to Chippenham to give a longer braking distance, as the diesel engines then in use tended to go faster than steam locomotives.

Left: Thingley Junction signal box – up branch distant signal "fixed at caution"; a lower arm was Lacock signal box –up starting signal until Lacock box closed

Below left: Thingley Junction signal box – Down branch starting No.45

Below right: Thingley Junction from Lacock bridge showing signal No. 45 in old position before being repositioned when Lacock came about in 1938. This signal was renewed again in November 1956

Thingley Junction signal box – top arm is down branch starting signal No. 45, the lower arm is Lacock down main distant signal No. 67

In quiet periods on the night duty I would sit down and then become aware of the odd sounds. Looking around a mouse would be running over the lino flooring its tiny claws making a faint noise, picking up a crumb or two before popping down the slot in the frame; good entertainment.

There was always plenty of wild life to watch outside of the signal box as it was surrounded by lovely countryside mainly farmland, with many birds throughout the year. Partridge in spring seemed always to be running up and down the path alongside the down main. Why they chose this particular spot I've no idea.

The cuckoo while here in summer called through a good part of the night as well as daytime. Sparrows made good use of the finials on top of the signal posts for their nests, an ever-changing scene.

One early morning I saw a fox with two cubs having a rough and tumble, a fantastic sight. On another occasion, looking over the field, I spotted a couple of hares boxing; not something one is in the habit of seeing, but the memory lasts a lifetime.

Sunsets varied of course, splendid and breath catching sometimes. In summer I saw the sun go down in the west and in a very short time saw it rise again in the east. In the middle of open country it was a very wonderful feeling to see these happenings.

Lightning can be very dangerous of course, but an awesome sight to watch it all around you from the windows of the signal box. When a storm was very near, it would pass through the instruments on the shelf above the frame. Occasionally it would ring the block bells. Being interested in nature, these were bonus moments.

On one occasion watching a down main train go by a youth was looking out of the window of the train. Suddenly he shot a staple about ½ inch long at me; it whizzed by my head; I found it on the floor later. I informed the Bath railway police who arrested the youth at Bath Station in possession of a catapult.

For a period of time the Berks and Hants line was closed for maintenance, this meant many of their trains were diverted via Westbury and Thingley Junction. This was a challenge, fitting them in with the regular trains. I really enjoyed doing this.

One Sunday morning I was working with Bathampton and Bradford Junction, I had accepted Billy Smarts Circus Special from Bathampton to stop at the 'home' signal. This signal was not outside the clearing point for the junction, so I had to stop the Circus train before I could lower the 'branch home' signal for a boat train – class 'A' head code - to proceed first. The circus train arrived but failed to stop at the 'home' signal. I pulled the detonator lever and the driver hearing the detonator brought his train to an emergency stop. I waved to the driver for him to set back outside the 'home' signal, which he did. The Boat train had stopped at the 'branch home' signal which was out the required distance. I then let it proceed without too much delay. The driver of the circus train was very worried - as so he should be. I told him I would not report it. In fact I heard nothing further about this incident.

Very occasionally a royal train would be scheduled; it would carry four head lamps on the engine, one on each bracket and also had two tail lamps on the rear coach. It would not be stopped if one lamp was out, or was missing; the next stopping place would be notified. The bell code for the royal train was 4–4–4 beats on the blockbells, normally for an express train the bell code was 4 beats only. At least two sections had to be clear ahead. Officials would be posted on the train, at some signal boxes, and certain places on route such as tunnels, stations and bridges. Arrangements would have been made for a marker to be placed on the platform for the engine to stop with the coach opposite where the royalty would embark or disembark the train.

Thingley Junction to Westbury a distance of nearly 14 miles was opened on 5 September 1848. The actual Junction was peculiar at that time in having no facing points on the main line, so trains for the branch had to stop and reverse into the down refuge siding, then forward to the branch on a line from the refuge. A short portion of this line towards the box stayed until it finally closed on the 24 March 1968.

Brunel had a prudent objection to facing points, especially at places away from stations where trains would pass at speed.

My collection of surplus railway equipment includes a wood cased distant repeater No. 52, which may be the repeater for the Thingley Junction Down main distant signal. I have connected it to a battery so it can still be operated. In the signal box it would be located on the block shelve above the levers, the pointer shows the position of the signal which is not visible from the signal box.

Wood-cased distant signal repeater No.52

Relief Signalman
1957 - 1959

When you became a relief signalman you could work in any box after learning for a while without having to go to Bristol each time, but you were subject to being passed out by the inspector first, and you would still have to be tested on the rules by the inspector periodically as well.

On 27 February 1957 I started as a relief signalman in Chippenham District - which also embraced Calne, Lacock, Melksham, Holt Junction, Langley Crossing and Dauntsey - mainly covering rest days. This was very satisfying as I went to a different box nearly every day. There were a few spare days for me, in which I could go to other boxes in the district and learn them for future coverage of work.

Devizes was interesting, being a single line and having a number of 'facing points' in the station. One day I walked through the tunnel, which was on the Patney side of the station, under the old Devizes Castle. The two signalmen there were box proud. The floor of the box was highly polished; so as not to spoil the surface the signalmen covered their shoes with dusters - I could not keep up with that one! One colleague of mine was sent to learn this box on a very stormy day; he was allowed only onto the doormat. The floor had to remain spotless whatever the weather or circumstances!

A free pass was given for use between Reading and Taunton as I could be called anywhere in an emergency - a small perk as it could also be used for private travel.

Lacock signal box

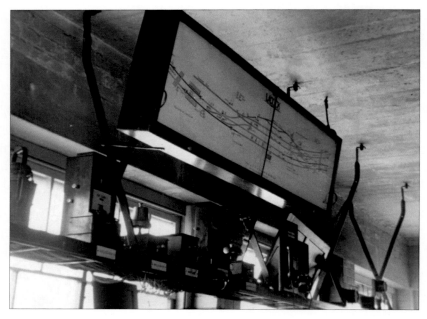

Lacock signal box signalling diagram

*Operating lever in
Lacock signal box*

Melksham signal box

*Melksham signal box
interior*

Calne Signal Box

Calne signal box

The signal box at Calne had a frame of 16 levers and a single line token instrument Calne to Chippenham, one platform and goods yard with several sidings. The platform was also used to load siphon wagons for Harris bacon factory. These wagons were sent to different parts of the country, some with boards on the side marked, for example 'Calne to Newcastle', 'Calne to Portsmouth' and 'Calne to Cardiff'. Smaller consignments were sent by passenger trains.

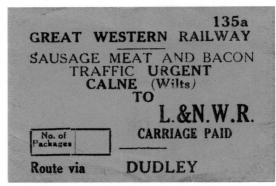

A G.W.R. label for what must be Harris Bacon Factory produce being transferred to L.&N.W.R via Dudley – the London & North Western Railway ceased operating on 31 December 1922

If any of these wagons were at the Calne platform, trains from Chippenham were accepted by the 'Section clear but station or junction blocked' bell signal 3-5-5 (warning arrangement); the train had to be stopped at the 'home' signal before we lowered the signal to the platform. All goods trains were to be accepted in this way before the facing points were reversed for the yard.

Calne signal box – distant signal

Note the temporary 20 mile per hour speed restriction –
this was a yellow arrow with 2 yellow lights

During the war thousands of RAF personnel for Compton Bassett camp and the aerodrome at Yatesbury came to this station; also parcels and freight for these camps. The coal merchants of Calne had their coal supplies come by train.

A two car auto train was mostly used, with engine and coaches at other times which had to run round to return to Chippenham. Signalmen Jack Kington and Arthur Iles were employed for the early and late duties.

While on night duty at Calne signal box my wife who was pregnant went into labour and was taken to St Martin's Hospital in Bath for her confinement. I had to remain in the signal box until a relief signalman arrived, before I could set off for Bath myself.

Calne station closed on 18 September 1965. The last passenger train from Chippenham to Calne and return was a Diesel Multiple Unit 3 car set, the driver was Frank Cannon, and the guard was Freddie Bond. Many people travelled on this train, I was one of them; the horn was constantly blowing and detonators exploding throughout the journey to Calne and the return to Chippenham. A large crowd was waiting on the platform for its return where a noisy reception was given with many more detonators going off. A wonderful farewell.

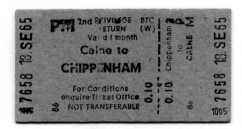

Tickets for last journey from Calne to Chippenham on 18 September 1965 – note time stamp 11.20 P.M. on the reverse

Calne signal box closed 2 November 1965. All connections were taken out of use and 'one train' working introduced. This was used for the Engineering Department to uplift the track.

As a relief signalman, I frequently worked at the little halt at Black Dog on the Chippenham to Calne Branch Line as the porter had retired from his post. In past times this was a busy little place, mostly with the movement of coal for coal merchant Heath of Derry Hill. While I was there sugar beet from the nearby village of Bremhill was the only large consignment of goods movement that I dealt with.

Years before, there was a siding used by the Marquis of Lansdowne, who had a private coach to attach to the train when needed. The cost of running the halt was paid for by the Marquis and was never in the public timetable. The points for the one siding were released from the ground frame by the single line token (Chippenham East – Calne). A General Post Office, G.P.O. telephone had been installed in the office; the public could use this, while the halt was open. One regular was the farmer who lived across the road.

Calne branch line 'Glass's Crossing' which allowed access to Joseph Glass's dairy farm at New Leaze Farm just outside Chippenham

Langley Crossing Signal Box

Langley Crossing signal box had a frame of 16 levers. There were only paraffin lamps for the crossing gates, so there was not much illumination for the public. It was a frustrating task to light these lamps when there was a high wind or gale. Unfortunately you could not light them in the box for as soon as you stepped outside the wind would blow them out! Even so, lighting them on the posts was still a problem; you certainly got through a number of matches and always needed to check there was a good supply in stock.

Langley Crossing signal box

Langley Crossing signal box – interior levers and hand wheel used to operate the crossing gates

Lighting for the box was a Tilley lamp, which gave a very good light. I often thought it would have been a great improvement if they had been used on the crossing but they never were. Drinking water was obtained from a stream nearby.

Langley Crossing – up main starting signal No. 6

Right: Langley Crossing – old distant signal No. 16 being dismantled

Below: Langley Crossing – new distant signal No. 16, this new signal was positioned further out so that the down main home signal No.15 could be further out to give adequate breaking distance for down trains

Dauntsey Signal Box

Dauntsey signal box had a frame of 37 levers and was on the Langley side of Dauntsey station where the junction for Malmesbury was situated many years before. The goods yard was on the upside, the Wootton Bassett side of the station. This meant the points for the yard were a long way from the box, so a ground frame was installed in a little hut. This had several levers including one for a 'crossover' between the up and down main. These levers were electrically released by levers in the signal box.

Above: Dauntsey signal box

Left: Dauntsey signal box – leaver, block shelve above and me

The 8.30 a.m. Chippenham non-stop to Swindon following the 7 a.m. Weston Super Mare to Paddington was a two coach set hauled by a tank engine which carried 'A' head code. The permanent way gang at Dauntsey called this train 'The Rattler' as it would be going flat out for such a little engine!

Wootton Bassett Incline signal box was taken out of use when the Intermediate Block Section (I.B.S.) was brought into use. This comprised a stop and 'distant' colour light signal in each direction; these were controlled from Dauntsey for the up main by a lever. When 'Line clear' had been received from Wootton Bassett West signal box and the train was passing the box, the 'Train approaching' 1–2–1 bell signal was sent. 'Train entering section', 2 bells, was not sent until the train passed the I.B.S. stop signal which would be noted by the ring of the lamp indicator in the signal box. The indicator had three positions: 'Off', 'Lamp out' and 'On'. The signal went from green to yellow for the 'distant' signal and green to red for the stop signal. The down main I.B.S. signals were controlled from Wootton Bassett West.

When single line working is in operation on double lines, a groundman is appointed to secure all 'trailing points' which would become 'facing' for trains to run in the opposite direction. This is done by securing the points with a metal screw clamp, which is held tight by turning the screw then securing with a padlock. Trains would have to set back through the crossover points.

Some weekends I worked as a groundman at different locations. One Sunday I was groundman at Dauntsey when the over bridge between the up and down platforms was being repaired, the downside in the morning with single line working between Dauntsey and Wootton Bassett West, the up line being used for both up and down trains. In the afternoon it changed over; with single line working Dauntsey to Langley Crossing on the down line. I was at this point appointed Pilotman wearing the official armband, which was red with white lettering. I would ride on the footplate with the driver of each train to go over the single line to Langley Crossing, but if another train was to follow in the same direction, I would show the first driver my pilotman armband, he would then proceed if signals were clear. I would ride on the last train in that direction. I would return on the next train from Langley Crossing. Again if there was more than one train coming up, I would ride on the last one to Dauntsey. The object of all this was to ensure that only one train was on the single line at any one time. Trains would have to reverse through crossover points to the opposite line to travel in the up or down line in the wrong direction. The pilotman's work on these occasions was to substitute for a normal single line token between the two signal boxes. While acting as pilotman I was thrilled to ride on the footplate of King George V 6000 from Dauntsey to Langley.

GWR Pilot arm ban used at Dauntsey

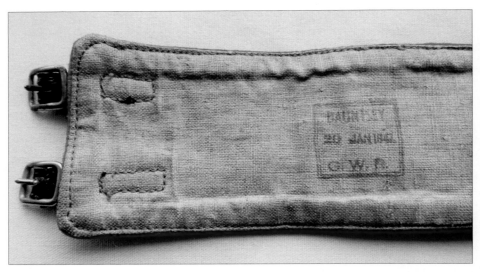

GWR Pilotman arm ban – date stamp on reverse side 'Dauntsey 20 Jan 1947'

Holt Junction Signal Box

Holt Junction signal box was between Melksham and Bradford Junction and had a frame of 49 levers. It was the junction for the Devizes branch which was worked by electric key token between Holt Junction and Patney. Quite a few trains used it going to and from the Berks and Hants main line at Patney as a route through to and from Trowbridge, Bath and Bristol via Bradford Junction.

I only worked this box for one week on the 6 a.m. – 2 p.m shift. Again I found it interesting to work yet another box.

Domestic Facilities in Signal Boxes

Most of the outlying boxes had buckets for toilets, which of course had to be emptied often. Digging holes were the order of the day to dispose of the waste. The signal boxes were mostly lit by paraffin lamps, which had to be filled and their wicks trimmed.

Some signal boxes had open fireplaces with the kettle sitting on the hob most of the time and an oven for warming food. Valour stoves were in some others for boiling the kettle. A supply of coal was allocated to each box but more was usually needed, so when an engine stopped near the driver obliged us with coal from his engine. Drinking water was obtained from a stream or a well; if this was not available, a can of water would be sent from a nearby station.

Thingley Junction Signal Box
1959 – 1964

The threat of redundancy came in the spring of 1959 when a decision was made to reduce the number of relief signalmen, fortunately there was a vacancy at Thingley Junction signal box and I returned there on Monday 13 April 1959 and stayed for over 5 years.

Thingley Junction signal box partially demolished after closing in 1968

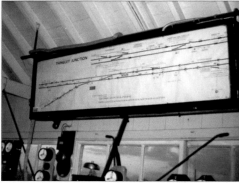

Thingley Junction signalling diagram

Chippenham East Signal box
1964 – 1966

On the 2 November 1964 I was back again at Chippenham East where I stayed for 2 years while new signalling was being extended to Thingley Junction. On 3 December 1966 Chippenham East closed, a very sad day for me.

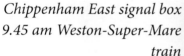

Chippenham East signal box
9.45 am Weston-Super-Mare
train

Chippenham East signal box
up main starting No. 57 and up
main to branch starting No. 54

*Left: Chippenham East signal box –
down main signal*

*Above: Chippenham East signal box
– Calne bay signal No. 43*

*Left: Chippenham East signal box –
down sidings signal No. 47*

Final Months
1966 – 1967

Following the closure of Chippenham East signal box I was sent to Corsham signal box until the new signalling extended to Bathampton and Bristol on the 25 February 1967. Corsham was my first and last signal box.

For a short while I was at Langley Crossing as there were new automatic half barriers installed. I was there to instruct the public how to use the crossing. It was probably while working there that I found an old memo dated 14 May 1897, giving a new instruction about the Sunday cover for Langley signal cabin to remain in circuit continuously. Another memo I found dated 20 December 1927 explained the procedure for sending time pieces for repair and how the keys should be attached.

After this I was back on Chippenham platform where I had started years before, sorting out redundant station equipment, from Melksham, Holt Junction, Calne and other stations which had already closed. All this equipment was then sent to Swindon. Dr. Beeching had been appointed to prune and make the railways pay. The whole system, signal boxes and branch lines, were all his victims. Not that the system ever was made to be profitable again. I too was one of those to fall under the axe and was made redundant. Finally I said goodbye to the railway on the 10 March 1967, having no regrets for what I had achieved over the twenty-five years.

Now getting on in years I walk along the road above the railway at Corsham towards the mouth of Box tunnel. I hear trains coming up out of the tunnel unseen as it is a very deep cutting and overgrown. Not quite the same as hearing the steam trains; nevertheless a reminder of very happy bygone days which I thoroughly enjoyed.

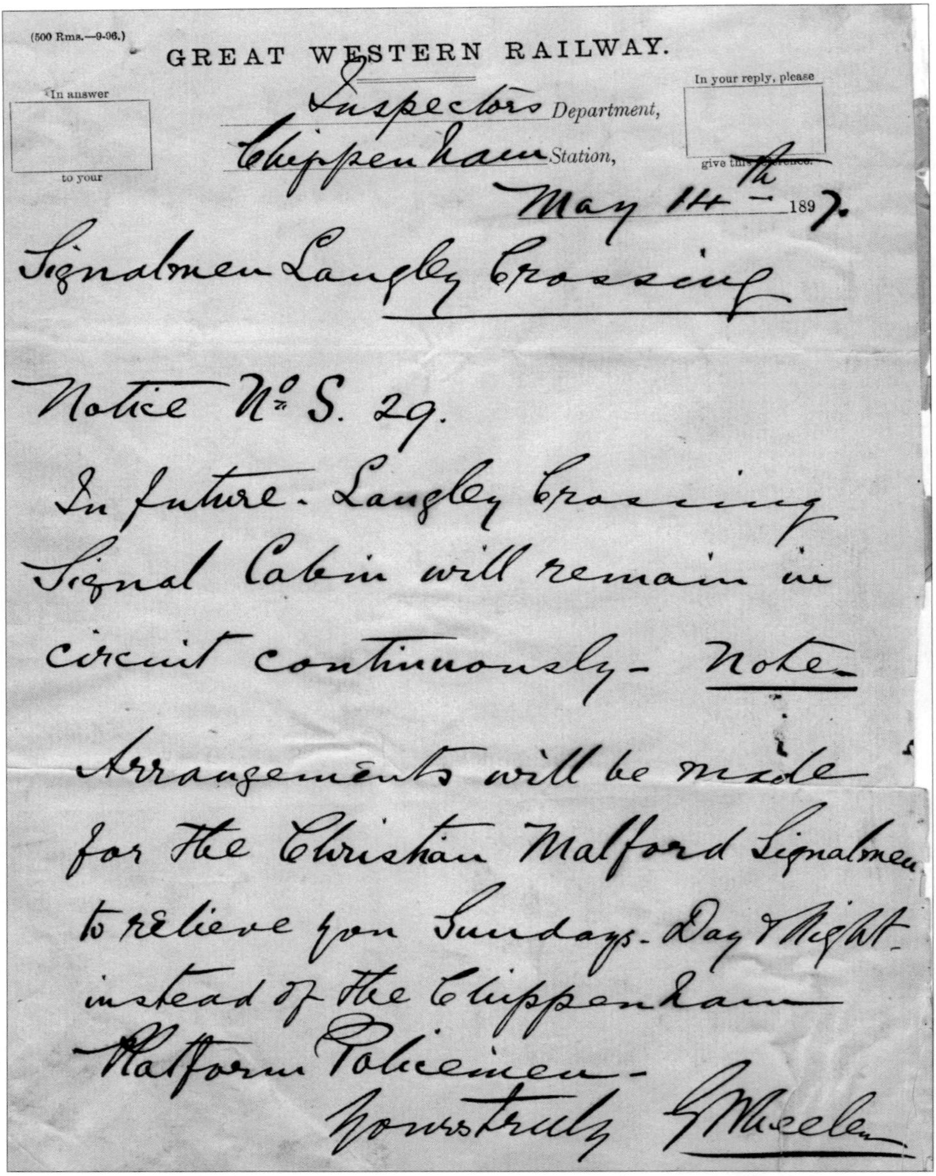

GREAT WESTERN RAILWAY.

Inspectors Department,

Chippenham Station,

In answer to your

In your reply, please give the reference.

May 14th 1897.

Signalmen Langley Crossing

Notice Nº S. 29.

In future - Langley Crossing Signal Cabin will remain in circuit continuously - Note

Arrangements will be made for the Christian Malford Signalmen to relieve you Sundays - Day & Night instead of the Chippenham Platform Policemen -

Yours truly, G Wheeler

Memo from Inspectors Department notifying that Langley Crossing signal cabin to remain circuit continuously – 14 May 1897

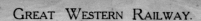

GREAT WESTERN RAILWAY.

Langley Crosslu

DIVISIONAL SUPT'S OFFICE.	STATION MASTER'S OFFICE,
Telephone— No. 14.	CHIPPENHAM.
B R I S T O L.	

Decr 20. 1927.

Please quote this reference—

Your reference—

WINDING OF TIMEPIECES.

It has now been decided to revert to the former practice of attaching the keys to timepieces when sending them for repairs and the same arrangement will follow in the forwarding of timepieces to stations after repairs. Please note and forthwith arrange for all keys to accompany timepieces forwarded for repairs.

The key of each timepiece must be attached to its ring handle and under no circumstances should it be placed in the cover of the clock.

If any difficulty be experienced in securing the key to a timepiece it should be enclosed in a Value envelope and forwarded to this office in due course with an explanatory note.

H.R.GRIFFITHS.

C O P Y. per W.C.

Memo about how time pieces and keys are to be sent for repair – 20 December 1927

My G.W.R. 'The ACME Thunderer' whistle which was with me throughout my time with the railway and lived up to its name making a very loud noise. My wife used to blow it when I was working on our allotment it to let me know when my meal was ready!

After leaving British Rail, I became a postman based at the Royal Mail sorting office which was situated next to Chippenham Railway Station at that time. The sorting office had a back entrance onto the station platform and I continued working there for nearly 24 years until my retirement.

Me at the Royal Mail sorting office Chippenham shortly before my retirement

Appendices

Appendix 1
The Brake Whistle

The big loud tone Brake Whistle still carried in addition to the ordinary whistle by all Great Western railway engines was introduced by Brunel and Gooch in the autumn of 1841 as a safety appliance to cause the instant application of brakes by the guard and generally to indicate danger. Its sound nowadays is confined to emergencies and is quite unmistakable. This applied only to G.W.R. steam engines.

Appendix 2
Great Western Railway Freight Journal

G.W.R. Freight Train Journal

Appendix 3

Wrong Line Working Forms

Great Western Railway Wrong Line Working Form A - Guard to Signalman prnted in pink paper

Form referred to in Rule 183, clause (f).   (1188)

GREAT WESTERN RAILWAY.
(A supply of these Forms must be kept by each Guard).

WRONG LINE ORDER FORM A.
GUARD TO SIGNALMAN.

To the Signalman at...signal box.

Allow an engine or breakdown van train to travel in the wrong direction to my train, which is stationary on the*.................................line at...............................

I will prevent my train being moved until the engine or breakdown van train arrives.

Catch points exist at.................................

Signed.................................Guard.

Date.................19......   Time issued.........m.

† Countersigned.................................

Driver of engine assisting in rear.

† Countersigned.................................

Signalman.

at.................................signal box.

* Insert name of line, for example, Up or Down Main, Fast, Slow or Goods.
† If necessary.

1,000 Bks., 12-lvs. and cover—Est. 658 (11)—10/37. S.

The Railway Executive Western Region Wrong Line Working Form B - Driver to Signalman printed on green paper and dated July 1949

(1189)

Form referred to in Rule 183, clause (g).

The Railway Executive
Western Region

(A supply of these Forms must be kept by each Driver.)

WRONG LINE ORDER FORM B.
DRIVER TO SIGNALMAN.

To the Signalman at.................................signal box.

Allow an engine or breakdown van train to proceed in the wrong direction to my train, which is stationary on

the*.................................

line at.................................

I will not move my engine in any direction until the arrival of the engine or breakdown van train.

Catch points, spring or unworked trailing points exist

at.................................

Signed.................................Driver.

Date.................19......   Time issued.................m.

†Countersigned.................................

Signalman.

at.................................signal box.

*Insert name of line, for example, Up or Down Main, Fast, Slow or Goods.
†If necessary.

Form referred to in Rule 183, clause (i).

(6974)

GREAT WESTERN RAILWAY.

(A supply of these Forms must be kept by each Guard).

WRONG LINE ORDER FORM **C.**
GUARD TO DRIVER.

To Driver of Engine No..............................

I authorise you to set back to the rear portion of your train.

Catch points exist at.............................

Signed...*Guard.*

Date ....19.........

Time issued...........m.

† Countersigned.............................
Driver of engine assisting in rear.

† Countersigned.............................

Signalman.

at.............................signal box.

† *If necessary.*

750 yads 12 lvs. and cover N.B./4—1939—(5) S.

*Great Western Railway Wrong Line Working Form C –
Guard to Driver printed on white paper*

(1190)

Form referred to in Rules 175, clause (c), 183, clauses (f) and (g), 184 and 203.

GREAT WESTERN RAILWAY.

(A supply of these Forms must be kept in each Signal Box).

WRONG LINE ORDER FORM **D.**
SIGNALMAN TO DRIVER.

To Driver of Engine No..............*working*.............................*train.*

I authorise you to travel with your train on the *.............................line in the wrong direction to this signal box.

Catch points exist at.............................

Signed.............................*Signalman.*

at.............................signal box.

Date.............19.....

Time issued.........m.

† Countersigned.............................

Signalman.

at.............................signal box.

* *Insert name of line, for example, Up or Down Main, Fast, Slow or Goods.*
† *If necessary.*

200 Bks., 12 lvs. and cover—Est. 777 (11), 12/37. S.

*Great Western Railway Wrong Line Working Form D –
Signalman to Driver printed on yellow paper*

Appendix 4

Signalling diagrams

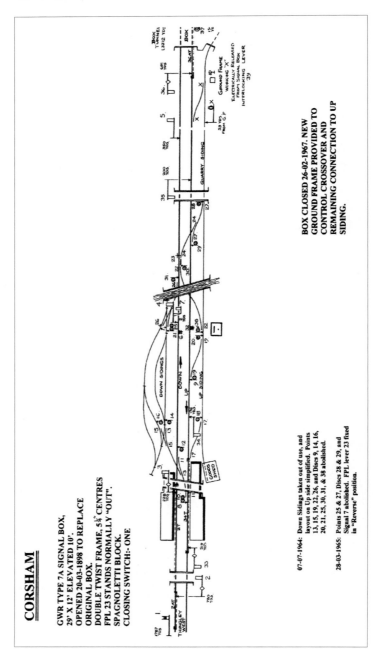

Drawing showing signalling layout at Corsham drawn by George Pryer and reproduced here with the kind permission of Signalling Records Society (www.s-r-s.org.uk)

Corsham Signal Box Levers

1. Down main distant nos. 23, 5, 4, 3, 2
2. Down main home
3. Down main inner home no. 23
4. Down main starting no. 23
5. Down main advance starting – 'Line clear'
6. Disc main detonators
7. Down main to up siding starting
8. Disc for no. 17-17
9. Disc for no. 19-19
10. Disc for nos. 11-23, 11-27, 24-11, 13-11, 13-15
11. Mains to cross
12. Disc for no. 11-11
13. Nos. 1 and 2 Down sidings to up main no.11
14. Disc for nos. 13-11, 13
15. No. 3 Down siding to up main
16. Disc for nos.15-11, 13, 15
17. Up sidings to up main
18. Disc for no 17-17
19. Up sidings to up main
20. Disc for no.19-19
21. Disc for nos. 26-23, 26, 27, 24
22. Up sidings to down main
23. Facing pint lock for nos. 24-27, 24-nil
24. Down main facing to up siding no. 27
25. Disc for nos. 26-23, 26
26. Down siding to down main
27. Up siding to up main
28. Disc for nos. 27-27, 27, 24, 26-27,11,12
29. Disc for no 27-27
30. Disc for no 22-22
31. Disc for no 26-26
32. Up main detonators
33. Up main advance starting – 'Line clear'
34. Up main starting
35. Up main inner home
36. Up main home
37. Up main distant
38. Disc for nos. 23-23, 22
39. Interlocking lever with Corsham ground frame – Electric switch

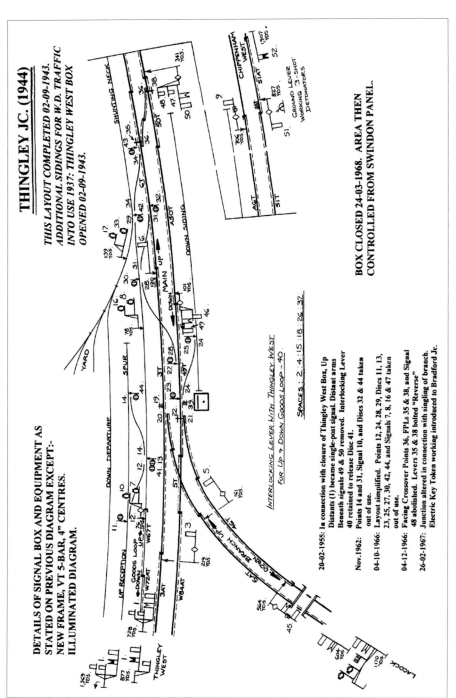

Drawing showing signalling layout at Thingley Junction drawn by George Pryer and reproduced here with the kind permission of the Signalling Records Society (www.s-r-s.org.uk)

Thingley Junction Signal Box Levers

1. Up main distant
2. Up main home
3. Up main inner home
4. Up branch home
5. Up branch inner home
6. Up main starter
7. Up main advance starter
8. Up main to up loop
9. Spare
10. Spare
11. Spare
12. Spare
13. Up detonators
14. Down main to up main disc
15. Down main to up loop disc
16. Down main to up main points
17. Up main to up loop
18. Up main to down main disc
19. Down main to down main signal
20. Branch to up main points
21. Down main facing
22. F.P.L. (facing points lock) for 21
23. Disc for 24
24. Down main down refuge
25. Disc for 24
26. Disc for 28 down main to up main
27. Disc for 28 down main to up siding
28. Points down main to up siding
29. Disc for 28 siding to down main
30. Spare
31. Spare
32. Disc at 28 to down loop
33. Signal - yard or loop to up main
34. Points - yard to main or from loop
35. F.P.L. (facing points lock) for 36
36. Crossover main to main
37. Disc for 34 up main to yard or loop
38. F.P.L. (facing points lock) for 36
39. Signal – down main to loop or yard

40. Down detonators
41. Spare
42. Spare
43. Spare
44. Spare
45. Down branch starting
46. Down main branch inner home
47. Down main advance starting
48. Down main starting
49. Down main inner home
50. Down main intermediate home
51. Down main home
52. Down main distant

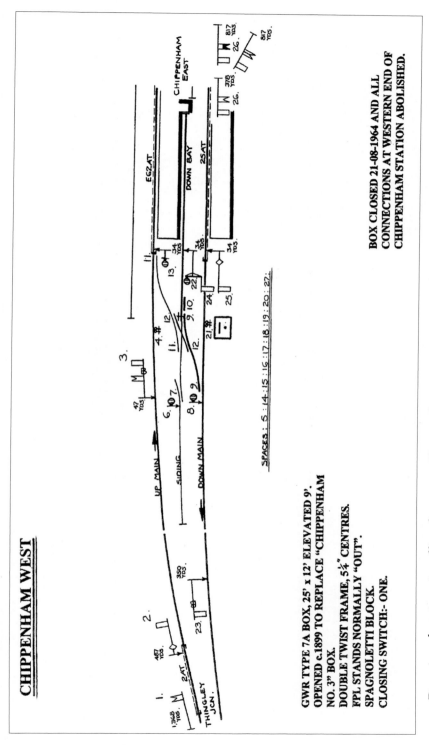

CHIPPENHAM WEST

GWR TYPE 7A BOX, 25' x 12' ELEVATED 9'.
OPENED c.1899 TO REPLACE "CHIPPENHAM
NO. 3" BOX.
DOUBLE TWIST FRAME, 5¼" CENTRES.
FPL STANDS NORMALLY "OUT".
SPAGNOLETTI BLOCK.
CLOSING SWITCH:- ONE.

SPACES: 5.14:15:16:17:18:19:20:27.

BOX CLOSED 21-08-1964 AND ALL
CONNECTIONS AT WESTERN END OF
CHIPPENHAM STATION ABOLISHED.

Drawing showing signalling layout at Chippenham West drawn by George Pryer and reproduced here
with the kind permission of the Signalling Records Society (www.s-r-s.org.uk)

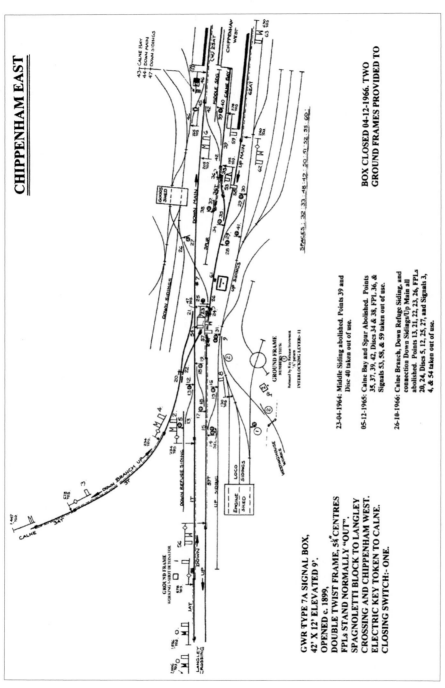

Drawing showing signalling layout at Chippenham East drawn by George Pryer and reproduced here with the kind permission of the Signalling Records Society (www.s-r-s.org.uk)

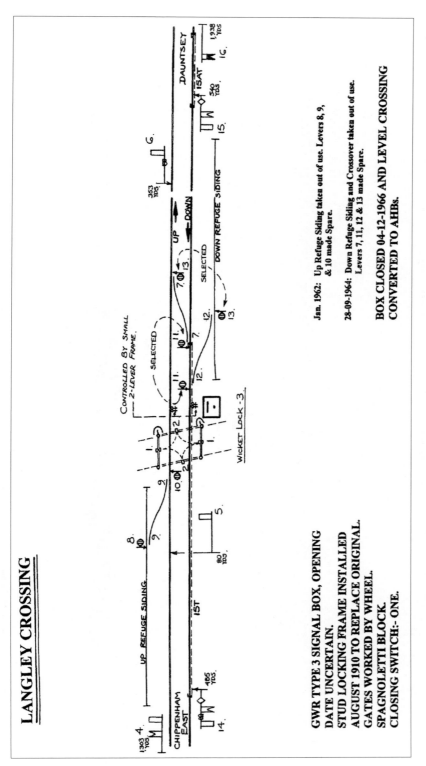

LANGLEY CROSSING

GWR TYPE 3 SIGNAL BOX, OPENING DATE UNCERTAIN.
STUD LOCKING FRAME INSTALLED AUGUST 1910 TO REPLACE ORIGINAL.
GATES WORKED BY WHEEL.
SPAGNOLETTI BLOCK.
CLOSING SWITCH:- ONE.

Jan. 1962: Up Refuge Siding taken out of use. Levers 8, 9, & 10 made Spare.

28-09-1964: Down Refuge Siding and Crossover taken out of use. Levers 7, 11, 12 & 13 made Spare.

BOX CLOSED 04-12-1966 AND LEVEL CROSSING CONVERTED TO AHBs.

Drawing showing signalling layout at Langley Cossing drawn by George Pryer and reproduced here with the kind permission of the Signalling Records Society (www.s-r-s.org.uk)

Appendix 5

Bell Codes

CODE OF BELL SIGNALS to be used in describing trains in No. 1 Column of the Train Register Book

Note.—In addition to inserting the Bell Signal, Signalmen should enter any further information which may be necessary to identify the particular train, such as "starting point", "starting time", "name of train", "time train is due", etc.

CLASSIFICATION AND IDENTIFICATION INDICATORS AND HEAD LAMPS

Class of Train (New)	Class of Train (Old)	Classification Indication (New)	Classification Indication (Old)	Description of Train	Special Classification Number	Bell Code
1	A	1		Express passenger train or Newspaper Train .. Breakdown van train or snow plough going to clear the line, or light engine going to assist disabled train .. .. Officers' Special train not requiring to stop in Section	— / 1Z99 / 1Z01	4 Consecutively
2	A	2 §§		Ordinary passenger train of a local character running under semi-fast or express conditions	—	4 Consecutively
		§ Last two digits in the block 00–49 (route number)				
2	B	2 ••		Ordinary passenger train, mixed train .. .. Breakdown van train NOT going to clear the line Branch passenger train (where authorised) .. Diesel Rail Bus	— / 2Z99 / — / 2Z01	3—1 / 3—1 / 1—3 / 3—1—3
		* Last two digits in the block 50–99 (route number)				
3	C	3 ¶¶		Parcels, fish, fruit, horse, livestock, meat, pigeon or perishable train composed entirely of vehicles conforming to coaching stock requirements ..	—	1—3—1
		¶ Last two digits in the block 00–49				
3	C	3 ••		Empty coaching stock train (not specially authorised to carry Classification "1" or "A" headcode)	—	2—2—1
		* Last two digits in the block 50–99 (route number)				
4	C	4		Express freight, livestock, perishable or ballast train pipe fitted throughout with the automatic brake operative on. not less than half of the vehicles	—	3—1—1
5	D	5		Express freight, livestock, perishable or ballast train partly fitted with the automatic brake operative on not less than one-third of the vehicles .. .. Elliott Track Recorder when not recording ..	— / 5Z08	5 Consecutively
6	E	6		Express freight, livestock, perishable or ballast train partly fitted with not less than four braked vehicles next to the engine and connected by the automatic brake pipe	—	1—2—2
				Express freight, livestock, perishable or ballast train with a limited load of vehicles not fitted with automatic brake	—	1—2—2
				Weed killing train when both running and spraying .. .. Matisa Track Recording Car when not recording	6Z07 / 6Z08	1—2—2 / 1—2—2

Any other specially authorised bell signals should also be inserted as required in column 1

Above and overleaf: Code of Bell Signals used to describe trains

CODE OF BELL SIGNALS to be used in describing trains in No. 1 Column
of the Train Register Book (continued from page 2 of cover)

Note.—In addition to inserting the Bell Signal, Signalmen should enter any further information which may be necessary to identify the particular train, such as "starting point", "starting time", "name of train", "time train is due", etc.

CLASSIFICATION AND IDENTIFICATION INDICATORS AND HEAD LAMPS

Class of Train		Classification Indication		Description of Train	Special Classification Number	Bell Code
New	Old	New	Old			
7	**F**	7		Express freight, livestock, perishable or ballast train not fitted with automatic brake	—	3—2
8	**H**	8		Through freight or ballast train not running under Class "4" ('C'), "5" ('D'), "6" ('E') or "7" ('F') headcode	—	1—4
				Train which can pass an out-of-gauge or exceptional load similarly signalled on the opposite or an adjoining line	8Z02	2—6—1
				Train which cannot be allowed to pass an out-of-gauge load of any description on the opposite or an adjoining line between specified points ..	8Z03	2—6—2
				Train which requires the opposite or an adjoining line to be blocked between specified points ..	8Z04	2—6—3
				Trolley requiring to go into or pass through certain tunnels	8Z05	2—1—2
				Lennox-Lomax earth auger machine, Matisa or Plasser automatic tamping machine not stopping in section	8Z06	1—4
				Matisa or Elliott Track Recording Car when recording	8Z08	1—4
9	**J**	9		Mineral or empty wagon train	—	4—1
9	**K**	9		Freight, Mineral or ballast train stopping at intermediate stations	—	3 Consecutively
				Branch freight train (where authorised) ..	—	1—2
				Freight, Ballast, Officers' Special train, Lennox-Lomax earth auger machine, Matisa or Plasser automatic tamping machine, requiring to stop in section	9Z01	2—2—3
0	**G**	0		Light engine or light engines coupled	—	2—3
				Engine with not more than two brake vans ..	—	1—1—3

Any other specially authorised bell signals should also be inserted as required in column 1

Appendix 6

Western Region W.R. Telephone Circuit No. 119

May, 1952.   8946
W.R. TELEPHONE CIRCUIT NO. 119
SWINDON - BRISTOL.

STATION	SEL. CALL	
Swindon Jc. Telegraph Office	5	1
" West Box	8	1
" Exchange	7	1
Dauntsey S.M.O.	4	3
Christian Malford Halt	4	5
Chippenham M.P.D.	4	4
" East Box	6	2
" Shunters	1	1
" Goods Office	2	4
* " Booking Office	6	4
" Ticket Collectors	1	3
" Per. Way Inspr.	1	4
" West Box	2	2
Thingley Junction Inspector	4	1
Corsham S.M.O.	5	4
Box S.M.O.	2	3
Bathampton S.M.O.	4	2
Bath Inspectors	6	1
" Telegraph Office	5	3
Bristol Exchange	3	1

*Switch to Chippenham - Calne
circuit No.242.

Appendix 7

One of the redundant items I purchased fropm British Rail was a large metal notice which allowed the fox hunt to use a level crossing to cross the railway line. The notice reads:

GREAT WESTERN RAILWAY

NOTICEIS HERE BY GIVEN THAT THIS LEVEL CROSSING MAY ONLY BE USED BY MEMBERS OF THE BADMINTON HUNT AND MEMBERS OF THE VALE OF WILTSHIRE (CIRENCESTER) HUNT AND OTHER PERSONS WHEN HUNTING WITH EITHER OF THE AFORESAID PACK OF FOX HOUNDS ON HORSEBACK OR ON FOOT (BUT NOT WITH WHEELED VEHICLES) DURING THE HUNTING SEASON AND THAT ALL SUCH PERSONS USING THIS GATE AND LEVEL CROSSING DO SO AT THEIR OWN RISK AND RESPONSIBILTY IN ALL RESPECTS AND SHALL NOT HAVE RIGHT OF ACTION CLAIM OR DEMAND AGAINST THE COMPANY BY REASON OF ANY DAMAGE OR INJURY WHATSOEVER WHICH MAY HAPPEN TO SUCH PERSON OR PERSONS OR HIS HER OR THEIRHORSES OR HOUNDS WHILE USING THIS GATE AND CROSSING

SEPTEMBER 1901
BY ORDER